WATER PLANET STORE

WELCOME! THANK YOU FOR COMING TO OUR SHOP TODAY! THIS BOOK YOU ARE LOOKING AT JUST NOW, DEBUTED IN 2000. IT'S A CATALOG OF CREATORS' WORK. THE THEME IS "WATER", WHICH IS THE ORIGIN OF CREATION. IT WILL BE PUBLISHED THREE TIMES A YEAR AS A SERIES. YOU CAN FIND THINGS YOU WON'T SEE ANYWHERE ELSE, AS WELL AS LIMITED EDITION PRODUCTS. THERE ARE MANY PRODUCTS WITH THE THEME OF "WATER" CREATED BY ARTISTS FROM VARIOUS FIELDS OF ART. YOU CAN BUY THESE PRODUCTS. PLEASE FILL OUT THE POST CARD AND SEND IT TO US IF YOU ARE INTERESTED IN PURCHASING ANY OF THESE ITEMS. WELL, PLEASE ENJOY THIS BOOK!

LET'S BUY THE CREATIVE POWER!
WATER PLANET STORE©

indispensable

000 EAST & WEST
-01/LUNCHEON MAT

001 YOSHIHIKO MAMIYA
-01/NINE RACK
-02/FRIENDLY

002 NAOKO HIROTA
-01/NAOCA BAG

003 SHUKUNO-RINTENDO
-01/AQUA-TRICK BOB

004 GENKOTU
-01/EH BIEN D'ACCORD

005 PAUL DALY
-01/TEAR AWAY

さて何本あるでしょう?

000-01/LUNCHEON MAT

Well, How many bamboo rods are there?

バ ラ ン ス 感 覚。 Keep balance

A wine rack. Bolts and its cubic form meet and support each other.
You will want to be particular about the wines to put in it.
When the roundness of fruit touches the bowl, it becomes a fruit bowl.
It has the refined beauty of the texture of natural wood and the curves are
picturesque without anything in it.

001-01/NINE RACK

001-02/FRIENDLY

002-01/NAOCA BAG
お買い物は何リットル?

水を得た自転車。
003-01/AQUA-TRICK BOB

1日1本、3日で3枚。
One bottle a day, three picutures three days.

004-01/EH BIEN D'ACCORD

Photograph by Ichigo Sugawara

365

Flush away the troubles.

二人のことは、水に流そうよ。

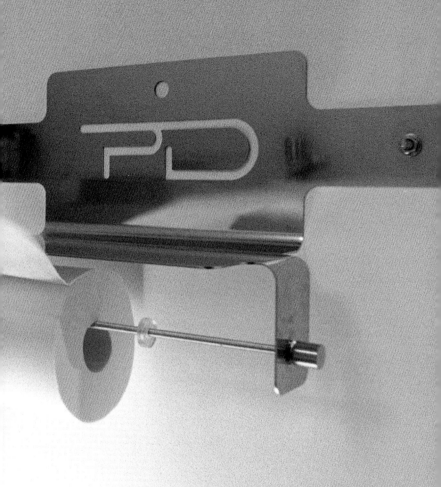

005-01/TEAR AWAY

Photograph by Yoshimi Kamada

000
EAST & WEST >>P128

風呂敷、畳、障子…。今、日本のトラディッショナルなモノの良さが改めて見直されている。暮らしがどんどん西洋化される中で置き去りにされてきた本物の良さ、実用性は時を超えて蘇生。和と洋、伝統と先進、その境界線にとらわれることのない若い世代のアーティストによって、現代空間にフィットする新しいプロダクトのカタチを見せはじめた。

000-01/日本の伝統工芸「簀巻き」と同様の編み込みを施したアクリル棒のランチョンマット。クリアで繊細なシンプル・ビューティーは和洋中、どんなテーブルコーディネイトにもフィットする。

Furoshiki (a square cloth for wrapping things to be carried), tatami (woven straw floor mats), shoji (paper-covered sliding doors), -- the merits of traditional Japanese things are now being recognized once again. The appreciation and the practicality of real things which were forgotten as our lives became more westernized, are brought back to life after many years. Japanese and western style, traditional and advance, are starting to show their new shape of products to fit into contemporary life by artists who aren't limited by traditional boundaries.

000-01/A luncheon mat of acrylic rods knitted together like Japanese sumaki (a small mat of rods of rattan used to make rolled sushi). Its clear and delicate simple beauty will fit Japanese, western, Chinese, or any style of table coordinate.

WATER PLANET STORE
purchasing information P.136

000-01 Luncheon Mat ¥3,000

01●素材／アクリルロッド　●サイズ／W400
D300 ●カラー／クリアー

001
YOSHIHIKO MAMIYA >>P128

ミュージアムに飾られたアートを眺めるのは楽しいけれど、創造的なフォルムと一緒に暮らし、身近に使いながら感じてみれば、さらに楽しい。機能と美を合わせ持つ家具。それは、アートと人との距離を埋めていく不思議なチカラを秘めている。

001-01/ボトルとキューブ状のフォルムが出会い、互いが互いを支えあうワインラック。並べるワインにもこだわりたい。001-02/果物の丸みとボールの形状が触れ合うだけで器として変身するフルーツボール。天然木の風合いと曲線が際立つ洗練美は、何ものせなくてもピクチャレスク。

It is pleasant to look at art in the museum, but it is even more pleasant to live with creative forms and use them and feel them. The furniture with function and beauty, it has a marvelous power to shorten the distance between art and people.
001-01 / A wine rack. Bolts and its cubic form meet and support each other. You will want to be particular about the wines to put in it.
 001-02 / When the roundness of fruit touches the bowl, it becomes a fruit bowl. It has the refined beauty of the texture of natural wood and the curves are picturesque without anything in it.

WATER PLANET STORE
purchasing information P.136

001-01 Nine Rack   ¥18,000
001-02 Friendly   ¥12,000

01●素材／ウォールナット　●サイズ／W330 D135
H330 ●カラー／ブラウン　●受注制作
02●素材／ウォールナット　●サイズ／W296 D209
H25 ●カラー／ブラウン　●受注制作

002

NAOKO HIROTA >>P128

「nAocA」ブランドのバッグはカバン屋やブティックでは購入することができない。販売されているのはいくつかの家具ショップとニューヨーク近代美術館 (MoMA) のみ。もともとインダストリアル・デザイン (ID) というフィールドで活躍していたデザイナーが、バッグに対する既成概念を取りはずし、コンセプトから素材、生産プロセスにいたるまでID的手法で手掛けるまったく新しいバッグ。カラダに触れ、ヒトの「持つ」「動く」といった行為によってしなやかにカタチを変え、完成される3次元曲面的なフォルムは、立体裁断されることによって身につける時も、そうでない時も常にキープされる。そしてそれは、すでにファッションとしてのバッグではなく、プロダクト・デザインとしてのポジションを獲得している。
002-01／ダイビングのウェットスーツ素材 (ネオプレーン) で作られたバケツ型バッグ。軽さ、丈夫さはもちろんのこと、水をシャットアウトするから雨の日のお出かけにも最適。

You can't buy [nAocA]-brand bags at bag shops or boutiques. They are only sold at a few furniture shops and at MOMA, the Museum Of Modern Art in New York City. Designers who originally worked in the field of industrial design threw away the stereotypical ideas of bags, and created from the concept of the materials and production processes of ID materials, so
these are completely new bags. Its three-dimensional form which changes its shape to conform to your actions, as when you carry it or when you put it down, is accomplished by three-dimensional cutting. It has already acquired the position as a product-design, not as a fashion handbag.
002-01/ A bucket-shaped bag made of neoprene, a material for diving wet suits. It's of course, light and strong and waterproof, so it's good for a rainy day.

WATER PLANET STORE
purchasing information P.136

002-01 Naoca Bag   ¥15,000

01●素材／ネオプレーン ●サイズ／W200 D140
H350 ●カラー／ブラック・ピンク・パープル・ターコイズ ●受注制作

002-01
中はオーガンジー素材の巾着になっていて、ひもで絞れば中身はシークレットに。
Inside is an organdy drawstring bag; you can close it with the string to hide what's inside.

003

SHUKUNO-RINTENDO >>P128

昔、翼のついた自動車やタイヤのついた船を想像したことはなかっただ
ろうか。力学や実現性なんて関係なく、空想の世界はいつも自由で無限
だった。歳を重ねるごとに規制や常識に縛られ、夢見ることを忘れてしま
った私たち。たとえば自転車にロケットをつけてしまう。そんな少年の心を
持ったアーティストの登場は、あらためて夢みることの素晴らしさを思い
出させてくれる。

003-01／ペットボトルロケットを搭載した水力自転車は、あくまでも自転車
のメインエンジン、「人間エンジン」を元気にすることが狙い。ロケットの
パワーのみでは走れないものの、水が勢いよく噴き出すことで気分を高め、
コンディションをアップ。マッハのスピードで走れそう!?

003-01
水圧を利用したペットボトルロケット
は、かなりの噴射威力を発揮。
A PET-bottle rocket which uses
hydraulic pressure to emit a strong
jet of water.

Did you ever, when you were a kid, imagine a car with wings or a ship with tires?
The world of imagination is always free and limitless. It has no relation to
mechanics or reality. As we grow up, we become bound by regulations and
commonsense, and we forget how to dream. The appearance of an artists who still
has a child-mind remains you of how great it was.
003-01 / A water-powered bike with a PET-bottle rocket. It's the main engine of the
bike but its aim is to stimulate the "human engine". The rocket alone won't move
your bike, but the water blasting powerfully out the back of the rocket energizes you
and improves your biking performance. Maybe you can bike at Mach spped!

```
||
WATER PLANET STORE
purchasing information P.136

003-01
Aqua-trick Bob          ¥900,000

01 ●素材／鉄・ゴム・ポリエチレン ●サイズ／
W700 D1370 H1000 ●カラー／グリーン ●セッ
ト内容／本体＋ペットボトル9本 ●受注制作限定
1台 ※要面接
||
```

004
GENKOTU >>P129

私たちの生活のすぐ隣には、ささいなことかもしれないけれど、楽しいこと、かわいいモノ、気持ちいいことが、実はいっぱい。だけどいつも時間がなくてストレスだらけの私たちはそれを見落としたり、さっさと処分してしまったり…。たまにはささいなことをじっくり見つめてみる、心のゆとりを持つことも必要。そこに、感性や美意識を磨いてくれるとても大事なメッセージが詰まっているかもしれない。
004-01/365本の潰れたペットボトルを日めくり写真集に。どれひとつとして同じモノがない多彩な表情は、ションボリしてたり、笑って見えたり、いろんな想像を膨らませてくれる。

There are lots of simple joys, little treasures, and other minor things that happen everyday which can make us feel good. They might be insignificant things, but they are right there in front of us, though we usually miss them because we are too busy and have too much stress. We should try to make time to relax and look around; to 'stop and smell the roses'. We might be able to find some very important messages to improve our sensitivity and sense of beauty.
004-01/ A 365-day desktop calendar pad with photos of squashed PET bottles. None of the bottles look the same; some look sad, and others look happy. Their expressions expand your imagination.

WATER PLANET STORE
purchasing information P.136

004-01 Eh Bien D'accord ¥5,000

01●サイズ／W100 D130 H70 ●受注制作限
定2001個 ※メーカーより許可が得られない場合、
もしくは注文規定数に満たない場合は製作されな
いおそれもあります。

004-01
日めくりはもちろん、ミニレターやメ
モパッドとしても活躍。
It can be used as a memo-pad.

005
PAUL DALY >>P129

アイデアやヒラメきが欲しい時、人知れず泣きたい時、ヒトはトイレに向かう。最もプライベートで心落ち着く小さなスペース。誰にも遠慮することなく自分の気持ちと向き合えるヒミツの空間。ついついおざなりになりがちだけど、もっともっと遊んだり、インテリアにこだわってみてもいいかも知れない。涙も、悩みもすべて水に流して、晴れ晴れ、新鮮な気持になれるように。
005-01/ "TEAR AWAY"と名付けられたステンレス製のトイレットペーパー・ホルダー。モダンで洗練されたテイストが、手を伸ばすたびやさしく心をなごませてくれる。

People go to the bathroom when they need to get ideas or inspiration, and when they want to cry without being noticed. It's the most private little place where you can relax. You can face yourself without worrying about other people. You might not care very much about how your bathroom looks, but it would be nice to be more particular about your bathroom's interior, to make it a pleasant place to flush away your tears and troubles, and to refresh your feelings.
005-01/ This is a toilet paper holder named "TEAR AWAY". Its modern, sophisticated style will comfort you every time you touch it.

WATER PLANET STORE
purchasing information P.136

005-01 Tear Away   ¥. カクヨミテイ

01●●素材／ステンレス・スチール ●サイズ／
W410 D230 H120 ●受注制作 ※価格未定

transparent and colorless

006   **NOBUHIKO SUZUKI**
-01/KEMURITOKEI
-02/KARAJIKAN

007   **SHINICHIRO ARAKAWA**
-01/WATER CLOTH

008   **THIS IS IT.**
-01/HANGING TABLEVASE
-02/OIL LAMP
-03/DOT PLATE
-04/PETRA VASE

006-01/KEMURI TOKEI

Glass balls lined up like water drops on frosted glass take on
the role of lenses, and looking through them delicately changes the
striped pattern on the face of the clock. This is a surrealistic,
unique clock which makes you forget about time.

006-02/KARAJIKAN

A shell, a button, nuts -- The clock with pieces of dreams in glass which, only by looking at it, takes you back to the innocent times you used to have when you were a child.

kaleidoscope

memory

water drop

006-02／貝殻、ボタン、木の実…。ガラスの中に夢のかけらを閉じ込めた時計は、眺めているだけで子供の頃の無邪気な時間に連れ戻してくれる。

006

NOBUHIKO SUZUKI　>>P129

レンズの始まりは、水のしずくだったらしい。水滴を通して見る風景。それは複雑にきらめき、ゆがんで見えたり、揺らめいたり、大きくなったり、小さくなったり…見る角度によって微妙に屈折し、表情を変える。その小さな宇宙に広がっているのは、水滴を通してしか見ることのできない無限の世界。もしも、その中に自分だけの宝物や大切な思い出をしまっておけるとしたら、どんなにかステキだろうか。きっと、そこにとじこめられたモノたちは永遠に色あせることなく、いたずらに変化を繰り返し、まるで万華鏡のごとく心をときめかし続けてくれるに違いない。

The origin of the lens seems to have been a water drop. The view you get looking through a water drop is intricately reflective and sometimes warped. Move, and the image becomes bigger or smaller. The image changes delicately depending on your angle of view. This is the unlimited world you can only see through a water drop. How nice it would be if you could keep your treasure or memory. Things put in a water drop would never fade and keep changing their expressions like a kaleidoscope to flutter in your heart forever.

006-01／すりガラスの上に、まるで水滴を落としたように並ぶガラスの球がレンズの役割を果たし、そこからのぞく文字盤の縞模様がデリケートに変化。時計でありながら、時を忘れさせてくれるシュールな逸品。

WATER PLANET STORE
purchasing information P.136

006-01 kemuritokei　¥12,000
006-02 karajikan　¥58,000

01●素材／ハンダ・ムーヴメント・ガラス・ポリエステルレジン ●サイズ／W145 D50 H185 ●カラー／無色 ●セット内容／本体＋乾電池 ●受注制作限定10個
02●素材／ガラス・ポリエステルレジン・ムーヴメント・木・ミクストメディア ●サイズ／W215 D30 H45 ●カラー／無色 ●セット内容／本体＋乾電池 ●限定1個

img:0033

img:0887

img:0088

img:0095

mg:0948

img:0922

007 >>P129
SHINICHIRO ARAKAWA

ファッションとは人が服を着ることに限らない。
水に着せるための服があってもおかしくない。そ
んな自由な発想から生まれたモード写真。Tシャ
ツを人間以上に上手く着こなす水の姿に、見る
ものは、ただただ嫉妬するばかり。007-01／無
色透明シンプルを極めたTシャツが、四季折々
の水面風情と自然に解け合うフォト。新しいの
に懐かしい、そんな感情を喚起する写真5枚。

img:0053

WATER PLANET STORE
purchasing information P.136

007-01 Water Cloth   ¥6,000

01●素材／プリント ●サイズ／キャビネ版 ●セット内容
／5枚組 ●限定10個

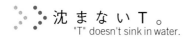

沈 ま な い Ｔ 。
"T" doesn't sink in water.

007-01/ WATER CLOTH

"Fashion" doesn't only mean the clothes that people wear. It's not strange that there are clothes for dressing water. This photograph was taken in such a spirit of conceptual freedom. People would feel envious when they see water looking much better wearing a T-shirt than humans do.
007-01/ The T-shirt is made of nylon. You can see how the simplest white T-shirt made of synthetics blends with nature and the water's surface with the flavor of the four seasons in these photographs. These five photographs are modern, but they give you a feeling of nostalgia.

浮かべる石。
Floating stones.

Photograph by Nob Fukuda

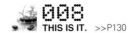

水は環境に応じて液体、固体、気体とカタチを変え、さらに波紋を描いたり、丸いしずくになったり、実に多彩で豊かな顔を持っている。決して永遠には留めておくことのできない、はかなく、繊細な自然のアート。水が織り成す一瞬一瞬の表情をカタチに残せたら…。限りなく水に近い人工の宝石、ガラスの魔法がそんな願いを実現してくれる。

008-01/シンプルなスタンドに支えられ空中に浮かぶ花瓶は、まるで水そのものが器として浮かんでいるかのような透明感。008-02/波紋をそのまま凍らせたようなガラス板と、その下に揺れるオイルのハーモニーが絶妙の美を醸し出すオイルランプ。008-03/水滴のテクスチャーをガラス上に表現。ランチョンプレートだけでなくアクセサリーや小物入れにも。008-04/花の色彩、水の表情を際立たせる無色透明のフラワーベース。石のホルダーで茎を支えるため、花を傷つけることもない。

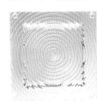

008-02
暗闇で灯すと光の揺らめきがガラスの波紋に波及して、より一層幻想的。
The sheet of rippled-glass is even more fantastic in the dark with a wavering light shining on it.

Water really has various faces which can change itself to liquid, solid, or vapor, and it also can make a ripple or become a water drop. It's never the same;---- fragile and delicate natural art. If you can create expressions of water and keep them... Artificial jewels which are completely water-clear: Glass magic will make your wish come true.

008-01/A vase floating in the air supported by a simple stand which has such perfect transparency that the vase itself is nearly invisible when filled -- you only see floating water. 008-02/The oil lamp: A sheet of glass like a frozen ripple and oil wavering underneath make a superb harmony to produce beauty. 008-03/Water-drop texture on glass: It can be used as a place mat or as a jewellery box. 008-04/The clear, colorless flower vase makes the flowers' color more conspicuous and is an expression of water. It has a stone holder to support the flowers which won't bruise them.

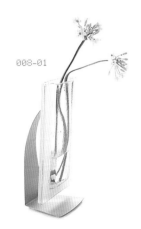

008-01

008-03

WATER PLANET STORE
purchasing information P.136

008-01
Hanging Table Vase(64T)   ¥9,900
008-02 Oil Lamp(511)   ¥7,000
008-03 Dot Plate(SW10D)   ¥4,500
008-04 Petra Vase(PV13)   ¥15,700

01●素材／ガラス・金属 ●サイズ／W114 D114 H260 ●カラー／クリアーグリーン×シルバー ●セット内容／ガラス製花瓶＋金属製スタンド ※簡単に洗浄ができます。
02●素材／ガラス ●サイズ／W165 D165 H25 ●カラー／クリアーグリーン ●セット内容／ガラス製プレート＋ガラス製小皿＋ランプ芯＋説明書
03●素材／ガラス・石 ●サイズ／W254 D178 H20 ●カラー／クリアーグリーン
04●素材／ガラス・石 ●サイズ／W200 D290 H50 ●カラー／クリアーグリーン×鉛色 ●セット内容／ガラス製トレー×1＋石×3

008–04
PETRA VASE

NO SPECTATORS

BURMA

世界に挑むウォータープラネットパフォーマンス

アメリカネバダ州の砂漠で開催される世界的に有名なアートイベント「バーニング・マン」。
毎年9月の第1週、世界中からアーティストが集まるこのインスタレーションイベントに
日本から初めてWATER PLANETが参加。
「砂漠にうるおい」をテーマに1週間のパフォーマンスを行った。

A world famous art event called 'Burning Man' is held in the desert in Nevada, U.S.A. In
the first week of each September, artists from all over the world gather to join this installation event.
We did a one-week performance with the theme of "moisture in the desert".

あっつ〜い!なんだ、このキョーレツな日射し!あまりの暑さで目が覚めた。朝がない。太陽が上がったら、いきなり昼。照りつける日射しのため、日中の気温は40℃以上にもなる。過酷な一日の始まりだ。そう、僕ケン・ハマザキは編集長の命を受けてこのとんでもないイベントにやってきたんだった。同行したカメラマンのヴィンセントが「レイヴなんか近くでやってい

たらうるさくて寝られないから、閑静な住宅地を早く探そう。都会の近くはトイレが混むむ」と言う。都会というのは、バーニング・マンの正面にあるセンターキャンプのことだ。ここには水やビール、ジュースなどドリンクだけが飲めるカフェやトイレ、ゴミ置き場のほかに、個人のイベントやパフォーマンスの日時を知らせる掲示板があちこちにある。いわば、町の役場のような場

Oh, It's so hot! the sun is so intense! I woke up because it was so hot. There is no "morning" here. Right after dawn, it's hot enough to be called "afternoon". It's time to start now. Yes, my name is Ken Hamazaki. I came to this unbelievable event for the editor-in-chief, Vincent, a photographer, said, "We should find some place quiet. I can't sleep well here because the Rave parties are so

noisy, and the restrooms are always busy near 'the city'. 'The city' is the center camp in front of Burning Man. There is a cafeteria, restrooms, a garbage dump, and many bulletin boards which tell you the schedule of events and performances. 'The city' can be compared to a city hall. We looked for a campsite. The speed limit is 20 kph. From my car window, I could see so many people. Everyone was

所なのだ。僕らは、時速20キロ以下(と車は決められている)でのろのろとテントを張る場所を探した。周囲を見ると、みんな思い思いのコスチュームに身を包み、自転車や車も盛大にドレスアップ。キャンピングカーで来ている優雅なやつもいる。ボディペインティングをしている女の子たちが何人も集まって自転車で行進していた(後で聞くとこれもパフォーマンスの一

種で、掲示板でメンバーを募集するらしい)。確かに自転車の方がよっぽど速いし移動に便利。センターキャンプで地図をもらう。イベントのシンボル、バーニング・マンを中心にしてパフォーマンスをしていい場所、入ってはいけない場所、テントを張ってもいい場所が明記してある。中央にあるバーニング・マンは日時計にもなっているのだ!これは便利!

dressed-up in fancy costumes, and even cars and bikes were decorated. I saw people with luxurious motorhomes. Some girls wearing body paint were parading on their bikes. Later, I learned that this had been one of the scheduled events listed on the bulletin boards for new members. Bikes are more convenient than cars here. We got a map at the center camp. It showed us 'Burning Man',

the symbol of the event, in the middle, and it also showed us where we could perform, where we could camp, and also where we should keep out. The 'Burning Man' is also a sundial! It was great!

art performance

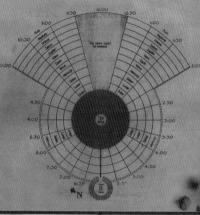

会場で見た数々の作品とアーティスト。どこでも好きな場所でくつろげて便利な移動式ソファに、ハエ男。目立つためには、とにかく高く見せること、竹馬蛾男。上が町の地図で時間や方角も分かる仕組み。

I saw so many works and artists; a portable sofa you can relax on anywhere, and Mr. Fly-man. To stand out, you have to be tall. It's a moth-man on stilts. Above is the map of the town, which shows you the time and direction.

バーニング・マンていったいなんだ?
What is the 'Burning Man' after all?

なんにもない広大な砂漠のど真ん中で行われるイベントの主催者は、ラリー・ハーベイ氏(51歳)。会場ではなんだかマッカーサーのようなスタイルだった彼が、失恋の悲しみを癒すためにサンフランシスコの海岸で20人ぐらいが集まり2.5メートル

The promoter of this event held in the middle of the desert is Mr.Larry Harvey, 51 years-old. He looked like MacArthur out there. The origin of this project was the party he held in San Francisco to comfort himself after he lost his girlfriend in 1986. He, along with 20 friends, burnt a 2.5-meter figure

の人形を焼いたのがプロジェクトの始まりだったそうだ。それが1986年のことで、1990年には現在のブラック・ロック・シティー、ネバダ州のリノから北へ200キロも行った砂漠地帯に場所を移し、燃やす人形も今では高さ15メートルの巨大なものになった。また集まった人の数も今回はなんと24,500人!毎年9月の第1週に1週間だけ行われる。町のゲートで100ドル

on the beach near San Francisco. In 1990, they relocated to Black Rock City, an area in the desert 200 km north of Reno, Nevada. Now, the figure they burn is 15 meters tall, and 24,500 people attended this year. This event is held the first week of every September, and anyone can join (for

Welcome to
We came here to do perform

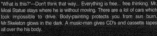

これはなに?なんて考えること自体がばかばかしくなってくる自由な発想。モアイ像のにいちゃんはずっとじっとして動かないし、ほんとに走れるの?という車もたくさん。ボディペインティングはキューリクな日射しから日焼けを防ぐためにも効果的なんだって、ガイコツ君は、夜になると発光して本領を発揮する怖さだ。CDやテープを全身に張り付けたミュージックマンも。

"What is this?"—Don't think that way... Everything is free... free thinking. Mr. Moai Statue stays where he is without moving. There are a lot of cars which look impossible to drive. Body-painting protects you from sun burn. Mr.Skeleton glows in the dark. A music-man gives CD's and cassette tapes all over the his body.

を支払えば誰でも参加できるが、原則として参加者はパフォーマーであること。1週間だけの町のシンボルであるバーニング・マンの周囲で、思い思いにパフォーマンスやインスタレーションを行う。そして、最後にはバーニング・マンと一緒に燃やしてしまい、後には何も残さない。ただそれだけ。かなりイカレてるボディペインティングの男も女も、合言葉は「Don't mind

a $100 entry-fee), but as a rule, you should be a performer. People are performing and doing installations all around Burning Man, and by the end of the week, everything is burned up with the Burning Man and nothing's left. That's it! Even crazy body-painted people give each other the

because of BURNING MAN!」。会場のあちこちで（本当に100ヵ所ぐらい）野外レイヴが行われているが、でも別に大物のDJが来るわけでもないから、そのひとつひとつに大勢の観衆が集まっているわけでもない。これがバーニング・マンを象徴している。観客はいない。楽しみは、とにかく個人主義なのだ!

password: "Don't mind because of Burning Man!" There are hundreds of raves being held everywhere, but none of the DJ's are famous, so there are no big audiences. This symbolizes Burning Man. No audience---only performance!

Black Rock City

ance to join in this unbelivable event.

SOLEMN

豊臣秀吉みたいに金の器でお茶を出したかった。きらきら光ってきれい？
I wanted to serve tea from a golden bowl like Hideyoshi Toyotomi did.

傘一本差した日陰、茶道の野点でチーン！
We had an open-air tea ceremony under a parasol for our performance.

9月3日と4日の2日間、野点をした。といっても、僕流のアレンジも入っているので、師匠に見られたら大目玉かも。なにせ、南堀江の山中大仏堂で買った仏前のチーン！を器にしているのだから。もちろん飲みほした後は、チーン！と鳴らしてあげた。この音が最高！からからに乾いた砂漠の空気にどこまでも響いて無常感が倍増なのだ。僕はこの野点のために、いろんなCDを選んで持っていったのだが、結局一番はまったのは、「聖なる水」という、水の流れと小鳥のさえずりだけが聞こえるもの。多くの人が、目を閉じたまんまじっとして、その居心地を楽しんでいた。みんなすごくイカれた格好をしているのに、畳の上に靴を脱いで上がると、すごく神妙な顔つきになって目を閉じ、何分間もそのままじっとしている。僕は実は吹き出しそうになるのをこらえるのが精一杯だったけど、こんな砂漠の真ん中でも、無の空間を作り出せる茶道って本当に奥が深いと改めて認識。ほんの一畳ほどの畳をしいた僕の空間だけが、砂漠の中にあって砂漠じゃない。わずかな間だけど永遠にひろがる、自分だけの宇宙観を感じてもらえたと思う。

We had an open-air tea ceremony for two days on September 3rd and 4th. My tea ceremony teacher might not be happy if she saw it, because it was my own style of tea ceremony. I used a bell from a Buddhist family altar as a tea bowl. I bought it at Yamanaka Buddhist goods shop in Minamihorie. After a customer finished drinking, I hit the bell and made a "ching!" sound. I love this sound. It echoes in the dry air in the desert. I felt transcendental. I prepared many CD's for our performance. The one I like best is called Sei Naru Mizu, "Holy Water", which only has sounds of a stream and birds twittering. Many people enjoyed this comfortably with their eyes closed. All of them looked so crazy, but once they got on the tatami mat, after they took off their shoes, they looked so serious and they closed their eyes and stayed there without moving. In fact, I nearly burst out laughing, but I realized how great the tea ceremony is, because it can create such a serious and comfortable air even in the middle of the desert. I had only one tatami, but it was a completely different type of space from the desert. I think that, for a short while, people could feel their own space which goes on forever.

こんなコスチュームの女の子が真面目に正座してお茶を飲む。
Girls in costumes like this sit upright very seriously and have a bowl of tea.

PERFORMANCE

さよなら、バーニング・マン
Good-bye Burning Man!

9月4日の夜8時か9時頃、バーニング・マンに火がつけられた。このイベントのクライマックスだ。あちこちで花火があがり、このときだけは、みんなが朝までずっと燃え続けるバーニング・マンの周りに集まってきて踊り出す。別にこれといって音楽はない。みんな適当だ。僕らの1週間もバーニング・マンと一緒に燃えつきるのだ。僕らの隣にテントを張っていたオーストラリア人の美大生も来ている。世界中の誰だか知らないけど、

このイベントに参加したみんなと一体になるのは、けっこう感動的。高さ15メートルのバーニング・マンも炎を上げて喜んでいるように見える。すごい迫力だ！凝縮したこの数日間がオレンジ色に染まっていく。すばらしいカタルシス！人生がリセットされる気持ちになる。生きる楽しみ（人生ともいえるかも）はとにかく個人次第、ということを僕は思いっきり目の前に突きつけられた。遠慮とか、図々しいとかいう考えは無用。誰にも迷

On September 4th at 8:00 or 9:00 PM, we set fire to Burning Man. This was the climax of the event. Everyone danced all night long around Burning Man, with lots of fireworks in the sky! There was no music. We burned up our week with Burning Man. I saw the Australian art university students who set their tent next to ours dancing, too. Being united with everyone who joined the event really

moved me. 15-meter-tall Burning Man seemed to be happy, too. It was very powerful. The firelight from Burning Man tinged our memory with orange. It was a wonderful catharsis. I felt like my life was reset. I learned that we are each responsible for making our own lives enjoyable. Forget about being reserved or shameless. Find your own way to enjoy your life without causing anyone trouble.

Good-bye Black Rock City
'Burning Man', one-week art performance
event, came to an end at last.

惑はかけず、自分がいちばん楽にいられるように自分の楽し
み方は自分で見つける。けっして他人に強要しない。それで
いて最高にハッピーな自分を演出する。それが、バーニング・
マンでのパフォーマンスだった。「ここには、60〜70年代の一
番自由で、みんなが平等だったアメリカのいいところが凝縮し
ている」とヴィンセント。彼は死ぬまで毎年、このイベントに参
加して、写真を撮り続けると言った。

Don't force anything on anyone, but make yourself happy.
That was the performance of Burning Man. Vincent said
"The best of the 60's and 70's from America, when
everyone was free and equal are condensed in this place."
He decided to keep photographing this event every year
until he dies.

ボク、ケンチャン。ボクとヴィンセントの作品を読者
の方にプレゼントします。P.139を見てネ。

Let's access

http://www.burningman.com

SHOP

PING

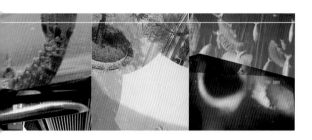

Christopher Doyle

director of photography

クリストファー・ドイルが手がけた、水のある風景

A waterscape produced by Christopher Doyle.

写真、コラージュ、インスタレーションなどの作品で独自の世界を表現してきたクリストファー・ドイル。
彼が監督したデビュー作品の "**AWAY WITH WORDS**" は
1999年のカンヌ国際映画祭にノミネートされ、世界中で公開された。
そんな彼から「僕の創造の根底にはつねに水がある」、
「だから、どれでも好きなものを選んでくれ」とのメッセージを添えて本誌宛にエクスプレス便が届いた。
今回、この「WATER PLANET」のために撮り降ろしてくれた作品の数々…。
彼の水への思いが伝わるメッセージも交え、改めて水が彼に大きく影響していると実感した。

Christopher Doyle has expressed his original vision in his photography, collages,
and illustrations. His debut work as a film producer, 'Away With Words', was an
official selection at Cannes 1999, and is in world-wide release. He said "'Water' is
always an underlying theme in my work, so please choose anything you like." That
was the message that came with his express parcel containing his work. He took
many pictures for this issue of WATER PLANET. We realized how much water
affects him when we read his message which tells us his feeling for water.

WATER PLANET（以下**WP**）今までの作品の中で水からインスピレーションを得たものはある？
クリストファー・ドイル （以下**CD**）水は、僕の創作活動に何らかのカタチで影響を与えていると
思う。僕が作る作品には、水をイメージの源としているものも少なくないからね。例えば「モーテ
ルカクタス」。韓国のパク・キヨン監督と組んだ映画は、孤独感が漂うモーテルカクタス407号
室で展開される4カップルのエピソード話。しずく、雨垂れ、泊まらないシャワー…。恋人たちはこ
んなにも水を求めていたと思わせる仕上がりになっている。けれど、目に見えるものばかりじゃない。
僕の作品は砂漠のイメージさえも水からきているんだ。水がないと言うことは、水を思い出させ
るからね。もっと言えば作品だけじゃない。僕自身のエネルギーにも水は大きく関係している。
英語には「脳に水」という言葉がある。僕は狂っているという意味だけれど、取り付かれたように
ひとつのことに没頭する。そんな風に集中して仕事をする時、僕はいつも海が見える場所にい
るんだ。海が持つエネルギーをもらうために。
WP 作品を作るにあたって、一番大切にしていることは何？
CD 人生においてもっとも大切なことを表現すること。僕にとって作品のイメージを作ること
はセラピーだと思っているんだ。自分自身に正直になって、シンプルに行動し、純粋な心で作
品を作ることは見る側にとっても、作る側にとっても癒しになると思うから。だから先入観もあ
まりもたないし、計画にもこだわり過ぎない。ただ今、目の前にある色や形が何を示しているか
だけを考えて心を開く。そうすることによって、初めて、作品は形になるものだからね。

WP（WATER PLANET） Is any of your work inspired by water?
CD（Christopher Doyle） Water affects my creative activity in some ways. Water has sometimes
been the source for my images. For example, "Motel Cactus". It's the story of four couples in room
407 at the Motel Cactus. It's a film about loneliness which was made in collaboration with Park
Ki-Yong, a Korean movie producer. Water dropping, rain-drops, and a shower that never stops ...
This film makes you think 'lovers yearn for water', but there are invisible things. In English they say I
have " water on the brain " (which means I am crazy). Water has been and remains so basic to my
life and energies, it will always be one of the most basic sources of my work: even an image of a
desert is informed by Water : its absence is its presence. Whenever I want to write or work in a
concentrated way I go to a place where I can see and get energy from the sea.
WP What is the most important thing when you make your art?
CD I think of image-making as " therapy ". It is what gets me closest to self and clarifies what is most
important in life : simplicity of act and purity of mind. Rather than going in with some preconceived
idea and plan I try not to think too much about what I am doing I try to be open to what a color or form
suggests, so that the work can somehow "find itself".

WP 最近の活動は？

CD 今はウォン・カー・ウァイと2本の映画の製作中。そのうちひとつは僕の人生のドキュメンタリーで、カンヌ国際映画祭に出品する予定。これは僕の祖国オーストラリアやその他数ヵ国で公開される。2月は香港でアニエスbとの展示会も開催。その後は世界中を旅しようかな。今?2本の新しいシナリオを執筆中。ビールも飲んでいるし、女性も大好きだよ。

WP 次はどんな作品を作りたい？

CD 写真家としても、映画監督としても、脚本家としても答えは同じなんだ。"より多くの人が楽しめる、優れた作品"。

WP 写真家として、撮影していて何が一番楽しい？

CD 普段はあまり気にしていない人やモノを、じっくりと見ることができること。

WP 写真家にとって一番大切な要素って？

CD 愛。これはとても広い意味で。僕は写真にアイデアとかテクニックとかが入り込むのを許したくない。シンプルで直接的で、ピュアであってほしい。そんな思いを含めて。

WP あなたの作品を愛する人たちに、何かメッセージを。

CD 行動あるのみ。私にできることは、必ずあなたにも出来るはずだから。

—— 今回の依頼に、情熱的な作品で応えていただいた彼の人柄に感動するとともに、心より感謝いたします。

WP What kind of work have you done recently?

CD I am still working on two films with Wong Kar Wai, one of which will go to the Cannes Film Festival, a documentary about my lifestyle about to be released in Australia and other countries. I have an exhibition with 'agnes b.', which is starting in Hong Kong next month, and then going on a world tour. I am writing two new scripts. I still drink beer and love women.

WP What kind of works would you like to make next?

CD My answer would be the same whether as a photographer, a movie producer, or as a screenwriter : Better works that more people can enjoy .

WP What can you enjoy the most when you take pictures as a photographer?

CD The thing I enjoy the most is that I can take a good look at things and people that I don't really care about in everyday life.

WP What is the most essential element for a photographer?

CD Love. I mean it in every sense of the word. I don't want to let ideas and technique interfere with the creative process. I want to keep my photographs simple, direct, and pure. I mean 'love' contains all of those meanings.

WP Do you have any message for people who admire your work?

CD Just do it : if I can so can you !

—— We are really moved by his personality and his wonderful photography, and we deeply appreciate his participation in this premier issue of WATER PLANET.

internet インターネットチャリティーオークション

Charity Auction Vol.01

「WATER PLANET AID」では、本誌のためにクリストファー・ドイル氏に創っていただいた作品のチャリティ・オークションをホームページ上で開催します。最高額で落札された方に作品を販売するとともに、その販売収益を日本ユニセフ協会を通じてチャリティします。

WATER PLANET will hold a charity auction on our home page. Mr. Christopher Doyle produced an original work especially for this auction. The winning bidder will be able to purchase this work, and the sales price will be contributed to UNICEF.

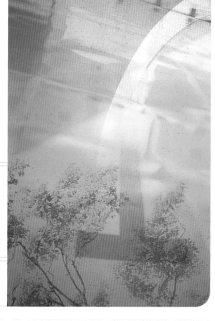

Piece of Work ▶ ▶ ▶
Original Print / Christopher Doyle
A4 size with frame
オークション出展作品
クリストファー・ドイルオリジナルプリント
A4サイズ程度、縦型フレーム付き

HOW MUCH IS IT?

オークションは本誌のホームページで実施します。
ご希望の方はご参加ください。
くわしくは>> http://www.pictogram.co.jp

実施期間:平成12年5月8日(月)〜5月13日(土)
結果発表:落札いただいた方に直接連絡します。また、落札いただいた方を本誌ホームページ及び2号の誌上で発表します。

The auction will be held on our homepage. If you wish to bid, please visit our website. Here is the link:
<http://www.pictogram.co.jp>

Bidding period From Monday, May 8th, to Saturday, May 13th, 2000, Japan Standard Time.
Announcement We will contact the successful bidder directly. Also, we will announce the result on our homepage and in the second issue of WATER PLANET.

009 **JUNZO KURODA**
-01/WASH MAN 2.0
-02/SENTOUKI (M)
-03/SENTOUKI (S)

010 **FURNITURE DESIGN AGRA**
-01/WHEEL
-02/WHEEL
-03/CHANGEABLE COVER

011 **SOUP DESIGN**
-01/WDH
-02/WDH S=1/10
-03/WDH S=1/10
-04/WDH S=1/10

009-01 / WASH MAN 2.0

009-01/ ブロックのように組み立て、ライト、スピーカー、水ホースなどのさまざまなアタッチメントを結合することで「洗う＋収納＋連結＋照明＋音響＋運ぶ＋遊ぶ」の機能を発揮。

009-01/ The sponges can function in various ways; they can be used for washing, storage, for connection, as a light, for sound, for carrying and for play, when you put them together like toy blocks and connect them to attachments like a light, speaker, hose, and so on.

Flexible Furniture
round frame chair & center chair

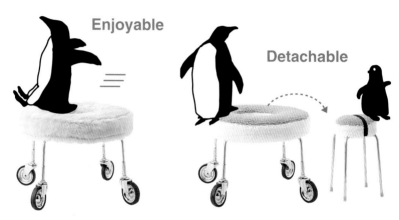

Enjoyable

Detachable

010-01.02 / WHEEL

 1. Enjoyable: A bigger chair with wheels. Discover your own way to play with it such as spinning around or rolling across the room.

 2. Detachable: You can take the small chair from the center and have two chairs; a big one and a small one. It's very convenient when you have a guest.

Changeable   Washable

010-03/CHANGEABLE COVER

 3. Changeable: Under the light-blue fake fur cover, there is another cover of stuffed-toy fabric. You can use a different cover in conjunction with the seasons.

 4. Washable: The fake fur cover is washable. You can always keep it clean and a beautiful color of blue.

 1.アソべる／大きい方の椅子はキャスターつき。クルクルまわったり、部屋中を滑ったり、いろんな楽しみ方を見つけよう。**2.わかれる**／センターの椅子を取り外すと大・小2つの椅子に変身。ゲストが来た時にもシェアできてとても便利。**3.着がえる**／水色フェイクファーの下にはぬいぐるみ素材のカバーがもう一枚。季節に応じて使い分けもOK。**4.洗える**／フェイクファーのカバーは洗濯可能だから、いつも清潔&きれいなブルーをキープ。

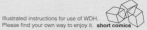

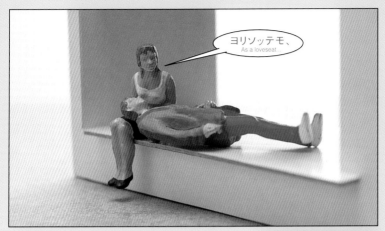

ヨリソッテモ、
As a loveseat...

カクレテモ、
As a screen...

トジコモッテモ、
As a hiding place...

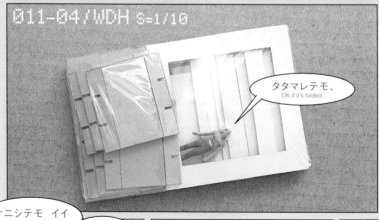

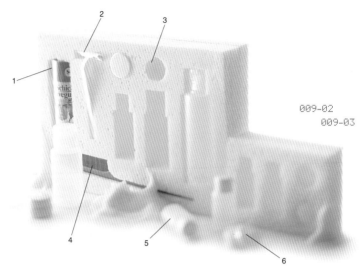

009-02
009-03

1.shaving cream
2.shaver
3.coin & minicase hole
4.hair brush
5.mini shampoo & conditioner
6.mini cream case

今回は販売しないけれど、薄いスポンジを
縫製した身体を洗える帽子「ライトセル」、
ブロックスポンジを組み立てたスーツ
「Washman 1.0」もラインナップ。
-Not available at this time- "Light Cell"
is a hat of thin, sewn sponge, which
can be used to wash your body. The
block sponge suit, "Washman 1.0" is
also on the list.

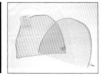

009
JUNZO KURODA

>>P130

いつの時代も、男の子なら一度は夢中になってしまうブロック。ただのデコボコしたピースを自由に組み合わせ、積み重ねることで、まったく新しいモノや思い描いたカタチを創り上げることができる、もっともシンプルでもっともクリエイティブなアソビ。子供だけのお楽しみにしておくなんて、もったいない。できないコト、あきらめだらけの現代社会。無限の可能性を持ったブロックなら、きっと大人のロマンも実現してくれる。009-01/不思議な空洞や凹凸記号がくりぬかれたスポンジは、洗える、拭けるだけでなく、シャンプーなどが収納可能。スピーカーを入れて音響器具に、ライトを入れて照明器具に…いくつでも、自由な形に連結させて好きなアイテムを創造できる。009-02・03/あらゆるお風呂アイテムが収納でき、洗える、拭ける、持ち運べるマルチスポンジ。銭湯はもちろん、海水浴やスポーツジムへも一緒に。03は旅行などに便利なパスポートサイズ。

In any generation, boys must have enjoyed playing with toy blocks. They stack the blocks up to build something completely different each time. It's the simplest and most creative toy. Adults should enjoy this, too. There are lots of things that people have to give up or can't do in today's society, but toy blocks, which have unlimited posibilities, can make adults dreams come true.
009-01/ Bumpy sponges with holes can be used to wash, wipe, and also can be used to store shampoo. It becomes a sound instrument when you put a speaker in it, and becomes a light stand when you put a light in it. You can create or build any shape or form. 009-02·03/ It is a multi-sponge. You can store bath items in it and you can wash with it, wipe with it, and it's easy to carry. Please take it to the public bath, to the beach, and to the gym. '03' is passport-size, a good size for travel.

I feel refreshed!

WATER PLANET STORE
purchasing information P.136

009-01	Wash man 2.0	¥4,000
009-02	セントウキ(M)	¥4,000
009-03	セントウキ(S)	¥2,000

01●素材／スポンジ ●サイズ／W260 D140 H120
●カラー／黄・ピンク ●セット内容／2個で1セット ●限定100セット
02●素材／スポンジ ●サイズ／W264 D180 H55
●カラー／黄 ●セット内容／本体＋空ボトル×3、クリームケース×2、シェービングフォーム、ひげそり、くし ●限定30個
03●素材／スポンジ ●サイズ／W90 D120 H40
●カラー／黄 ●セット内容／本体＋ボトル×2 チャームジャー×2 ●限定100個

010 FURNITURE DESIGN AGRA
>>P130

デザインから制作まですべて、原ななえ自身がこなすあぐら家具企画の椅子。ポップなデザインから雰囲気だけの家具と誤解しがちだけど、彼女がこだわるのはあくまでも椅子の座り心地であり、機能。フェイクファーを使うのも座り心地、肌触りが良く、洗濯できるという長所に着目したため。可愛さはもちろん、一度座るとその心地良さのとりこになってしまうことは間違いない。
010-01.02/池の水をイメージしたブルーと、川の水をイメージしたブルーの2バージョンを展開。010-03/別売りの着せ替えカバーで、自由にコーディネート。

The chairs of Furniture Design Agra are designed and created entirely by Nanae Hara. You might think they are only good-looking, pop-design furniture, but she is always particular about comfortableness and function. This is the reason she uses fake fur, which is comfortable to sit on, feels nice, and can also be washed. It is, of course, cute, and you'll never forget how good you feel if after sitting on it only once! You'll love it!
010-01.02/ There are two different versions. One is the blue color of pond water, and the other is the blue color of the image of river water. 010-03/Changeable cover for another coordinate.

```
WATER PLANET STORE
purchasing information P.136

010-01.02  Wheel      ¥55,000
010-03  Changeable Cover
                      ¥8,500

01.02●素材／ウレタン・フェイクファー・ステンレス
●サイズ／W500 D500 H350 ●カラー／ホワイト
&パウダーブルー・スカイ ●セット内容／センターチ
ェアー＋まわりのチェアー ●受注制作
03●素材／フェイクファー ●カラー／スカイ
●セット内容／センターチェアーのカバー＋まわり
のチェアーのカバー ●受注制作
```

011 SOUP DESIGN
>>P130

モノに支配されつつある私たちの生活。周りにあるほとんどのインテリアはすでにカテゴリー分類され、役割も決められている。だけど本当はもっと自由であるべき。想像力を膨らませてくれる家具。個々の生活サイズに合わせて使えるインテリア。そんな発想に可能性を見いだしたのが段ボール。水から生まれた素材でありながら、実は一番水がニガテというのもご愛嬌。011-01/"軽い、折り畳める、運びやすい"段ボール製の家具シリーズは椅子になったり、机になったり、使う人のサイズによって自由自在に機能。011-02〜04/ 1/10 サイズバージョンには、もれなくオモチャの人形つき。

Our life is becoming dominated by stuff. Most of the interiors around us are categorized and they are allotted a role, but they should be used more freely. The furniture which fires your imagination. The interiors which can be adjusted to an individual's personal size. Such an idea has found its possibility in corrugated cardboard. It's rather cute that water is its weak point even though it was made from water.
011-01/ Light, foldable and easy to carry, corrugated cardboard furniture becomes chairs, desks and other things. The furniture fulfills its function according to the user's size and purpose. 011-02~04/ The 1/10-size version comes with a toy doll.

```
WATER PLANET STORE
purchasing information P.136

011-01  WDH           ¥15,000
011-02~04  WDH S=1/10  ¥1,500

01●素材／ABボール（t=8mm） ●サイズ／
W850 D250 H850 ●カラー／段ボール素地 ●
セット内容／本体＋取扱説明書 ●受注制作（注
文総数が10個に満たない場合は、制作されない事
があります。）
02〜04●素材／白ボール（t=1mm）●サイズ／
02:W85 D25 H47.5  03:W65 D45 H85  04:
W70 D40 H70 ●カラー／白ボール素地 ●セット
内容／本体＋フィギュア ●限定／各タイプ5個
```

サイズ比率図 10:1

011-01

WDH   WDH S=1/10

011-02

W85 D25 H47.5

011-03

W65 D45 H85

011-04

W70 D40 H70

ミニチュア人形は何が付いてくるかは、解りません。

How high is the humidity?

012 **LOVE THE LIFE**
 -01/KTN 02/water
 -02/KTN 02/water
 -03/KTN 02/water
 -04/KTN 02/water
 -05/KTN 01/halo

013 PATRICK RIMOND
 MIZU-NO-TSUKI

014 **BENOA BERGER**
 -01/PAINTING
 -02/PAINTING
 -03/PAINTING
 -04/PAINTING

015 **TAKAO YAMASHITA**
 -01/GRAPHIC T-SHIRT+CD

016 **GRAF** DECORATIVE MODE NO. 3
 -01/LIGHT COSMO

017 **HIROYUKI NAKANO**
 -01/PEACEDELIC VIDEO
 -02/OPTRONIX

We've forgotten those wondering feelings since we've grown up. Sometimes we need to remember that innocence and become curious again.

部屋の中にみずたまり。
A puddle in the room

012-02/KTN 02/water

012-03/KTN 02/water

During the sunny autumn.
014-01/PAINTING

014-02/PAINTING

014-03/PAINTING

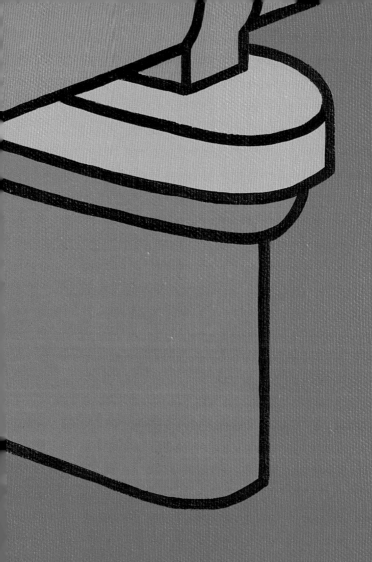

014-04/PAINTING

聴く
015-01/GRAPHIC T-SHIRT+CD

揺らぐ
016-01/LIGHT COSMO

映る

017-01/PEACEDELIC VIDEO
017-02/OPTRONIX

012
LOVE THE LIFE >>P131

子供の頃、水たまりを見つけると足をザブンと突っ込みたくなる衝動を抑えきれなかった。足と靴のすき間に入った、なま温かい水を踏みつける時の奇妙なカイカン。まるく広がり続ける波紋を見つめる無邪気な時間。大人になるたびに心の余裕を失い、すっかりご無沙汰になってしまったそんなイタズラ心やフシギ感覚。時には呼び覚まして、なにもかもに好奇心旺盛だったあの頃の自分を取り戻してみることも必要かもしれない。

012-01〜04/ビジュアルも触り心地もユニークな4種類のラグは、まるで部屋の床の上に水たまりができたり、水滴が落ちてきたみたいで、思わず歩くのが楽しくなってしまうデザイン。01・02は濃いブルーの部分に1センチほどのカットパイルを、薄いブルーのライン状の部分には7ミリほどのループパイルを植え、見方によっては部分的にまるく凹んで見えたり、出っ張って見えたり、視覚の錯覚を引き起こす。中央に大きなマルが見えるパターンと、サイドに小さいマルが見えるパターンの2バリエーションがラインナップ。03は白い部分が生地そのままで、ブルーの部分のみに短いパイルを植えたリズミカルな水玉模様。04は毛筆状のパターンが10色のパイルのグラデーションで描かれたジャパニーズ・テイストがインパクトあり。012-05/40ワットのサークライン蛍光灯をそのまま露出したミニマムなデザインの照明器具。ユラユラ揺らすと光輪の軌跡が暗闇に光の波紋を広げてくれる。

When we were kids, we used to have an impulse to stick a foot into a puddle of rainwater. We had a strange but pleasant feeling when we took steps with warm water in our shoe, and we kept looking at the ripples widening on the water. That was our innocent time. We've forgotten those wondering feelings since we've grown up. Sometimes we need to remember that innocence and become curious again.
012-01~04 / Four kinds of rugs which are visually and texturally unique are just like a puddle of spilled water on the floor in your room, and make you feel pleasant to walk on them. Numbers 01 and 03 have a one-centimeter cut-pile in the dark blue part and a seven-millimeter loop pile in the light blue part, which of course produces an optical illusion and makes them look like a round hollow or partial projection. There are two different variations. One has a big circle pattern in the middle, and the other one has a small circle on the side. Number 02 consists of two colors, white and blue. The white part is the color of the fabric and the blue part has a rhythmical polka-dot pattern made of short piles. Number 04 makes an impact with a Japanese-style pattern made by a gradation of ten different color piles which shows a pattern that looks like a brush drawing.
012-05 / This is a simply-designed lamp with an exposed forty-watt circular fluorescent light. When it swings, the tracks of the light create a ripple of light in the dark.

012-04

012-05

WATER PLANET STORE
purchasing information P.136

012-01~04
ktn 02/water   ¥65,000
012-05 ktn 01/halo ¥65,000

01〜04●素材／ウール100%●サイズ／W1500
D1500 ●カラー／01ブルー、02ブルー、03ブルー×
ホワイト、04グレイスケール ●受注制作
05●素材／スチール・電球色サークライン40W
●サイズ／R375 H350 ●カラー／クローム ●セ
ット内容／本体＋電球色サークライン40W ●受
注制作

013
PATRICK RIMOND >>P131

水なのに、水に見えない。見慣れた風景やありふれたモノもまったく違う表情になってしまう。それが、技術ではなく心で撮る彼ならではのファインダー・マジック。単なる時の記録ではなく、その場の空気感までが伝わる1枚1枚。そこには、まぎれもなく彼がレンズ越しに見つけた秘密の感動や街の鼓動が写っている。

013-01/あまりにも静かで優しい水の表情をとらえたオリジナルフォトをサイン入りフレームに収めて。見つめるだけで乾いたハートに潤いとぬくもりを与えてくれる。誰も知らない哀愁や力強さを切り取った街の横顔。選り抜きのポストカード5枚もセットで。

Water which doesn't look like water. Familiar views of commons things are changed to a completely different appearance. It is his finder-magic. He takes pictures with his heart, not by his technique. Each picture is not only a record of the time, but they give you a feeling of the air of the places. They show you a secret impression and a heartbeat of the town that he found through his lens.
013-01 / An original photograph which catches an expression of quiet and kind water in a frame with his autograph. When you look at these pictures, they give your dried heart moisture and warmth. Include five sets of postcards of towns which show you sadness and strength you've never noticed.

WATER PLANET STORE
purchasing information P.136

013-01 Mizu-no-Tsuki
+5 Postcards ¥42,000

01●素材/写真・木枠 ●サイズ/W570 D400
●セット内容/オリジナルフォト×1＋ポストカード×
5＋フレーム×1 ※限定20枚 ※送料込み

013-01

014
BENOA BERGER >>P131

彼の発想は、あくまでも自由。キャンバスに描かれた作品だからといって、"絵"として壁を飾るなんていう方程式は必要ナシ。ひとつの"オブジェ"として、裏向きに伏せて置いたり、横向きに立てて置いたり、感性のまま自由に楽しめばそれでOK。

014-01〜04/青く、流れの静かな水辺を描いた4つの光景。穏やかで心地よい気持ちに誘う抽象的なタッチは横からも、裏からも、もちろん正面からもサマになる。

His imagination is persistently free. There is no need for a formula that paintings done on canvas have to be hung on a wall as a "picture". You can place them face down, stand them sideways, or in any way you feel as objects d'art.
014-01〜04 / Four spectacles draw the blue, quiet flow at the water's edge. Abstract paintings which lead you to feel peaceful and comfortable can look good from the side, from the back, and of course, from the front.

WATER PLANET STORE
purchasing information P.136

014-01~04 Painting ¥12,000

014-01〜04●素材・キャンバス・アクリル ●サイ
ズ/W155 D18 H225 ●受注制作 限定各40枚

015
TAKAO YAMASHITA >>P131

岩にしみ入る清水のように、嵐の中の怒涛の洪水のように。色も形も変幻自在な自然の怪物、水。この特性を思考に置き換えるならば、"subconsciousness（潜在意識）"。柔軟に、でも多大に人の意識に訴えかける彼のアート。今回は人の脳にもっともダイレクトに侵入する"音"というモンスターに形を変えて登場した。

015-01/なぜか落ち着く雨の日。水をイメージしたオリジナルリミックスのCDは、そんな感覚に陥るアンビエントな1枚。流れる水滴が描き出すジャケットと同じデザインのTシャツとセットで。Tシャツの水滴部分には光る特殊な染料を使用。

Like spring-water which can soak into rock, like flood-water from a storm, a natural monster which is free to change its color and shape, --- water. If this feature of water could be put into word, the word would be "subconsciousness". His art appeals to people in many ways. This time, it has changed to a monster called "sound" which can go into your brain directly. 015-01/ I don't know why you can relax on a rainy day. This original remix CD with the image of water gives you such a feeling. It's ambient music. Glowing dye is used for the water drops. It comes with a T-shirt with a picture of a water-drop; the same design as on the CD jacket.

015-01

WATER PLANET STORE
purchasing information P.136

015-01
Graphic T-shirt+CD　¥8,000

01●素材／T-shirt：綿100% ●サイズ／S（身丈67cm、身幅48cm）・L（身丈73cm、身幅53cm）●カラー／黒・紺 ●限定200組 ※グラフィックはリフレクタープリント使用。プリントサイズ（315×315）、プリントの位置は表示レイアウトとは若干変更する場合がございます。

016
GRAF DECORATIVE MODE NO.3 >>P132

たとえば、夏の窓辺の風鈴。音だけで部屋に涼を呼び込む小さなインテリア。機能ばかりじゃない。本当に部屋に欲しかったものはそんな居心地の良さ。これがあるだけで部屋に水滴が落ちるような静寂が加わる。そんな快適さを作るインテリアをあなたの部屋にひとつ。

016-01/水面に石を投げ入れた時に広がる波紋。そんな自然の現象をインテリアとして自分の部屋に取り込めるシンプルなモビール。

For example, it's a wind-chime outside the window in the summertime. This small ornament can create a cool atmosphere with its sound alone. Function is not always the most important thing. What you really need is something which can make your room comfortable. This can add a silence like dripping water to your room. You should have one of these in your room.
016-01/ A ripple widening on the water when you throw a stone in it; this simple mobile brings such a natural phenomenon into your room.

016-01

WATER PLANET STORE
purchasing information P.136

016-01　Light Cosmo　¥38,000

01●素材／ステンレス・耐燃ペーパー ●サイズ／W800 D300 H400 ●カラー／白 ●限定10個

017
HIROYUKI NAKANO >>P132

人が生きるために一番大切なもの、それは水と酸素。すべての生命の源が故に、この2つに人は永遠に魅せられるのだろう。中でも魅力的なのが大自然が育んだ天然の水。究極の天然水、屋久島の水に虜になった人間が作った水の映像には、しぼんだ気持ちを蘇らせ、癒し、エネルギーをチャージさせる不思議な生命力が備わっている。

017-01/屋久島に何度も足を運び収録した30時間以上もの映像の中から、個人的に編集したプライベートな和みビデオ。小川のせせらぎから滝の流れまで、見るだけで心が洗われる水の映像。

017-02/OPTRONIXのDelic Disc第一弾。ハマる音楽と自然音によって森の奥や別宇宙への旅が可能。デスクトップでループすれば仕事中もリラックス。

```
▌▌

WATER PLANET STORE
purchasing information P.136

017-01 Peacedelic Video H2O
                     VHS  ¥3,500
                     DVC  ¥4,000
017-02 Optronix          ¥2,200

01●素材/VHS or DVC ●90分 ※受注制作
100本 ※VHSかDVCのいずれかをお選びください。
02●素材/CD ●限定500枚

▌▌
```

017-02
中野裕之プロデュースによる西芳宏と自然音のオーソリティー中田悟によるユニットOPTRONIX
'OPTRONIX' -- the collaboration of Yoshihiro Nishi and the authority on natural sounds, Satoru Nakata. Produced by Hiroyuki Nakano.

The things that humans need to live are water and oxygen. That is the reason why these two things are so attractive to people. The most attractive is pure water that comes from nature. The ultimate pure water is water from Yakushima. An image of the water there which was made by people who fell victim to its charms, can relieve people's distress and cure their minds and energize them. It has miraculous power. 017-01/ The original film is more than 30 hours long, which was made from their many visits to Yakushima. This one has been edited to capture the peaceful images. Your mind will be washed by a little stream and a waterfall. 017-02/ The first Delic disc from OPTRONIX. You will feel like you're travelling in a forest or outer space with this music and natural sounds CD. It can be looped onto your computer desktop, to help you relax while you're working.

017-01 ▶▶

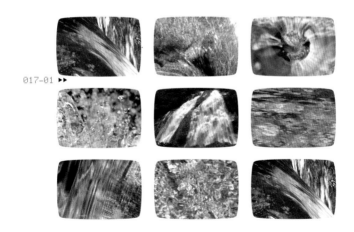

for people and also for fish

018 **SILICON BABY**
-01/LOVE LIP RING
-02/LACQUERED LOVE LIP RING
-03/SILVER TORSO

019 **EXIT METAL WORK SUPPLY**
-01/CAPSULE LIGHT JAMO 2000

020 **D.R.T,**
-01/NAKED FISH
-02/NAKED FISH
-03/NAKED FISH
-04/NAKED FISH

021 **HIROKO HOSOMI**
-01/LITTLE MERMAID
-02/NAGEOIRE
-03/NAGEOIRE
-04/UNI LAMP

022 **ATELIER SU:SO**
-01/TAMA TABLE LIGHT
-02/TAMA DAI
-03/TAMA FRAMES

023 **JONATHAN E. AKERS**
-01/SPUD MIRROR
-02/SPUD MIRROR
-03/POND TABLE

パーフェクトボディになる。
To become perfect body.

018-01/LOVE LIP RING

about 2ℓ
018-02/LACQUERED
LOVE LIP RING

Lungs Choker

Heart Ring

Liver Brooch

Stomach Pin

Large Intestines Bracelet

Small Intestines Necklace

Penis Ring

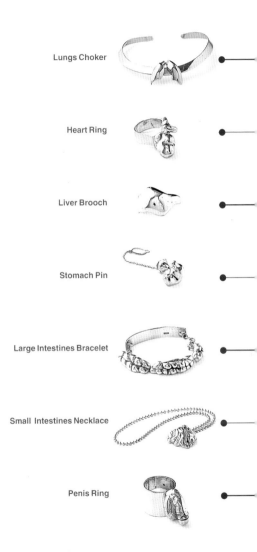

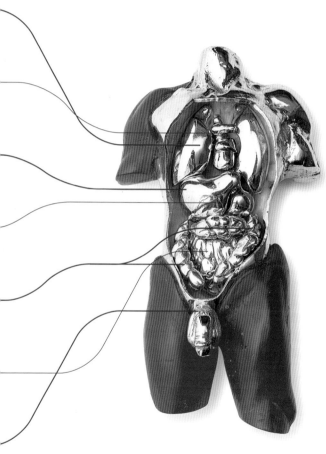

付属のチェーンや金具を
使えばアクセサリーが完
成。ちなみにフタの乳首
はピアスになっている。
You can make
accessories with a
chain and metal
fittings. The nipple-
shaped lids of the case
are earrings.

お茶する、薬を
飲む、食事する
などの行為によ
って、人は1日に
約2リットルの水分を摂取してい
る。また、血液、汗、涙、体液などを含めると人
体の約60%は水分。体重50Kgの人であれば
毎日、30Kgにも及ぶ水を背負っている
ことになり、もしその水を失えばヒトの体温は
100℃近くにまで上昇してしまう。
水なくしては成り立つことも、維持することもできない人体の神
秘、美しさ。それは神が創った、自然の造形美。唇、乳房、内臓
の一つひとつにいたるまで、生命力にあふれ、
力強く躍動するその輝きには決
してどんな高価な宝石もか
なわないだろう。
018-01・02/妖艶な唇型リングは01
がシルバー、02はシルバーの上に漆
でコーティング。018-03/シルバー
の人体ケースに、さまざまな内臓型
のパーツを内蔵。心臓はリングに大
腸はブレスレットに

People consume about two
liters of water a day by
drinking tea, taking medicine, and eating.
About 60% of the human body is water;
including blood, sweat, tears, and other body
fluids. The human body is about 60% water.
This means that for a person who weighs 50
kilograms, about 30 kilograms is water.
If all the water were to be removed from a human
body, the body temperature would go up
to 100 degrees Celsius.
Humans cannot survive without water.
The mysterious and beautiful human body
is a natural plastic art-work that God made.
No precious gem can compare with the energy
and brilliant life-force of each part of a human
body, such as lips, breast, and organs.
018-01・02 / This fascinating lip-
shaped ring, '01', is silver. '02' is covered
with lacquer.
018-03/ This silver human-body case has
various organ-shaped parts. The heart is a
ring. The colon is bracelet.

018

SILICON BABY >>P132

WATER PLANET STORE
purchasing information P.136

018-01 Love Lip Ring   ¥10,000
018-02 Lacquered
Love Lip Ring   ¥18,000
018-03 Silver Torso   ¥600,000

01●素材／Silver925 ●サイズ／W30 D30 H30
●受注制作 ※サイズは12号～20号のみ
02●素材／Silver925・漆塗り ●サイズ／W30
D30 H30 ●カラー／赤・ベージュ ●受注制作 ※
サイズは12号～20号のみ ※こちらの商品は漆の
完全乾燥のため、到着後最低3ヶ月間はご使用で
きません。また、アレルギー体質の方にはお薦めし
かねます。
03●素材／Silver925,950・アクリル樹脂 ●サイ
ズ／W70 D150 H50 ●セット内容／人体型ケー
ス×1＋choker×1＋ring×2＋brooch×1＋pin
×1＋bracelet×1＋necklace×1＋取付け金具
×1 ●受注制作限定10個

おやすみ前に…
Before going to bed...

Capsule Light *Jamo* 2000

Comes a unique blend of *Relaxation, Smart, Funny* and other important elements.

Weight : 737g / Size : wide-160 high-248 (depth-116 mm / Material : Aluminum & Brass / Capacity : 1.5V ...

(Mode : *Mood Light* / *With Case*

020-01/NAKED FISH

020-02/NAKED FISH

We used to really want to have magic items from the stories we read; like a magic wand or a magic lamp.
These items are made from bits of those children's stories as treasures for adults.
They have a wonderful power to reflect your childhood memories.

021-01/LITTLE MERMAID
021-04/UNI LAMP

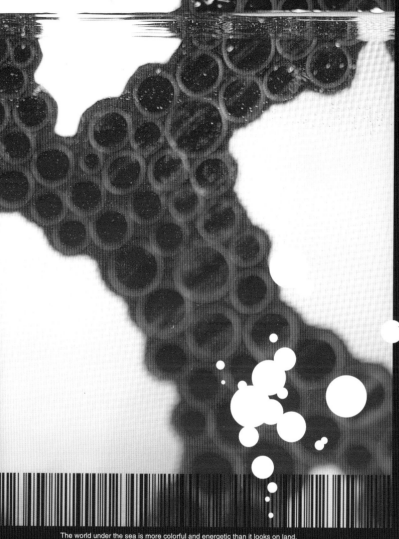

The world under the sea is more colorful and energetic than it looks on land.
Glowing creatures, a prism of sun and an eddy springs naturally... There is a lot of invisible power,
and people can't help being attracted to that marvelous power.

022-03/TAMA FRAMES

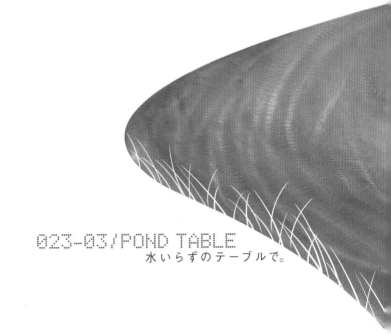

023-03/POND TABLE
水いらずのテーブルで。

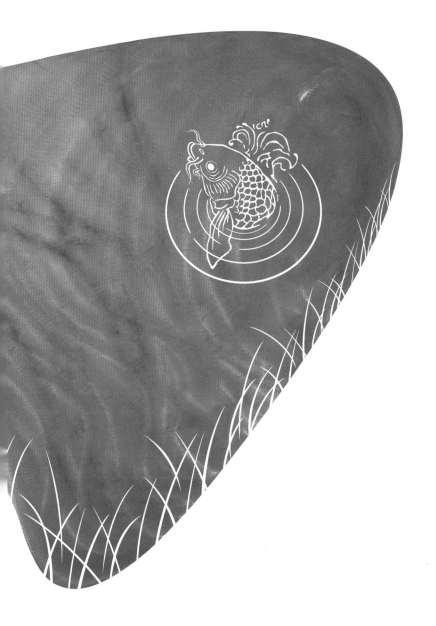

>>P132

019
EXIT METAL WORK SUPPLY

机の上に置かれていた風邪薬コンタック600のカプセルを眺めながら、メンバーの1人がつぶやいた。「カプセルの中に照明の光源を封じ込めた照明はつくれないだろうか。」毎日の生活の中から見つけだした小さなインスピレーション。そんな作品への想いを大切にするため、様々なリスクを覚悟で制作に取り組む。作品創りとはこんな純粋な想いがあってこそ、はじめていいものが生まれる。ちょうど、純度の高い水と一緒に飲んでこそ、薬が効くように。019-01/ たまたま机の上に置かれていた風邪薬、コンタック600が発想のルーツ。あくまでもリアリティを追求した照明は、クスッと人を笑わせる効果あり。朝と夜、就寝前に一日3回服用。

平面に置いても、壁にかけても使える
カプセルライトJamo2000
It can be used on a horizontal surface, or mounted on a wall. The capsule light "Jamo2000".

While looking at a cold-medicine capsule which was on the desk, one of the staff murmured, "I wonder if we can make a light which has an illuminant in the capsule.". It was a little inspiration found from an everyday object. We were determined to tackle this project at any cost, just out of feeling for our good products. Good products are produced from pure feelings, just like medicine works best with pure water.
019-01/ The cold-medicine, 'Contac 600'-capsule which happened to be on the desk was the origin of this idea. This realistic light will make people laugh to see it. To be taken three times daily; in the morning, in the evening, and just before bedtime.

WATER PLANET STORE
purchasing information P.136

019-01 Capsule Light
Jamo 2000 ¥29,000

01●素材／ポリカーボネイト・アルミニウム
●サイズ／W350 D250 H120 ●カラー／赤・青・黄
●受注制作

>>P133

020
D.R.T,

「この世でもっとも描くことが難しいもの、それは滝である。」そう言ったのは、かの思想家フランシス・ベーコン。昔から水はアーティストたちにとって創造への刺激であり、永遠のテーマでもあった。ベーコンのこの言葉に衝撃を受けて現在、水を作品に描き始めたペインター。水は時代を超えて人を刺激し続ける。水面に波紋が広がっていくように。
020-01〜04/ 赤い金魚が入った水槽の向こうにクラリネットを吹く自分の姿。水にゆがんで映る顔が立体的で、何ともリアルなアーティストの自画像。

The philosopher Francis Bacon said, "the hardest thing in the world to paint is a water-fall". Since time immemoriable, water has stimulated artists to create, and it's the eternal theme of art. Here is the painter who began to paint water after he heard the words of Bacon. Water crosses time to stimulate people just like a ripple spreading across the surface of a pond.
020-01~04/ The artist, playing the clarinet, reflected in the tank of red-gold fish. It's a very realistic self-portrait. The artist's face takes on a three-dimensional aspect caused by the water's warping of the image.

WATER PLANET STORE
purchasing information P.136

020-01.02 Naked Fish ¥60,000
020-03.04 Naked Fish ¥20,000

01・02●素材／キャンバス・アクリル ●サイズ／
W1300 H1700 ●受注制作
03・04●素材／キャンバス・アクリル ●サイズ／
W364 H515 ●受注制作

021
HIROKO HOSOMI

>>P133

魔法の杖やランプ。小さい頃、読んだ絵本
の中に登場したいくつものキラキラした魔
法のアイテム。それが欲しくて欲しくて仕方
がなかったあの頃の自分。そんな物語のカケ
ラを形にしたアクセサリーは、大人になっ
てもやっぱり宝物。幼い頃の思い出まで輝
かせてくれる不思議な力を持っている。
021-01/ 海の都・人魚王国。かつてその国
では太陽からの贈り物でたくさんの美しい
宝石であふれていた。そんなおとぎ話がル
ーツで生まれた深海に光るブレスレット。
021-02・03/ 太陽の恵みをたたえた首飾りは、
あまりの美しさに人間の心をも動かした。そ
んな言い伝えも納得できる人魚王国の姫・
Nageoireの首飾り。021-04/人魚王国の
宮殿にはきっとこんな照明があったに違い
ない。サンゴをイメージしたランプ。

We used to really want to have magic items from
the stories we read; like a magic wand or a magic
lamp. These items are made from bits of those
children's stories as treasures for adults. They
have a wonderful power to reflect your childhood
memories.
021-01/ There used to be an under-sea nation -- a
kingdom of Mer-people filled with beautiful jewels
from the sun. This shiny bracelet which invokes an
ocean abyss is inspired by this fairy tale.021-02·03/
This necklace celebrates the sun's blessing which
moves humans' hearts. You will believe this
legend when you see the necklace of the Mermaid
princess, Nageoire. 021-04/ There must be a lamp
like this in the kingdom of the Mer-people. This
lamp was made in the image of coral.

WATER PLANET STORE
purchasing information P.136

021-01 Little Mermaid (bracelet)
                    ¥38,000
021-02 Nageoire (H381N)
                    ¥13,500
021-03 Nageoire (H379N)
                    ¥13,000
021-04 Uni Lamp   ¥45,000

01●素材／ガラス・ピューター ●サイズ／全長約
210 ●限定1個
02●素材／ガラス・ピューター・天然石 ●サイズ
／全長約305 ●カラー／黒×ピンク×グリーン
●受注制作限定10個
03●素材／ガラス・ピューター・天然石 ●サイ
ズ／全長約360 ●カラー／黒×赤×ブルー
●受注制作限定10個
04●素材／ガラス・水晶 ●サイズ／W150 D200
H150 ●カラー／ブルー ●限定1個

021-02

021-03

021-04

021-01

022 >>P133
ATELIER SU:SO

海の中の世界は、地上から見るよりずっとカラフルで、エネルギーに満ちている。自ら光を発する生物、太陽のプリズム、自然発生する渦巻き…。目には見えないたくさんのパワー。そして、その不思議なチカラに人は魅せられずにはいられない。
022-01/刺激的な色使いや質感がSU:SOならではの、大胆奇抜な個性派テーブル。022-02/積み重ねると絵合わせが楽しめるイスは、オブジェにもなる3個セット。022-03/色鮮やかな"あぶく"がいっぱい。そんなプクプク感が楽しいフォトフレーム。3連タイプだからストーリー仕立ての写真やシリーズモノの展示にも最適。

The world under the sea is more colorful and energetic than it looks on land. Glowing creatures, a prism of sun and an eddy springs naturally... There is a lot of invisible power, and people can't help being attracted to that marvelous power. 022-01/Su:So is the only one who can create this sensational color and texture. A bold and original, unique table. 022-02/You can enjoy a puzzle if you stack these chairs. Good for objets d'art. Three chairs per set.022-03/This is a bubbly photo frame with lots of colorful bubbles. It's good for photos which are related to each other, or for exhibiting a series of photos, because it's a 3-photo frame.

WATER PLANET STORE
purchasing information P.136

022-01 Tama Table Light
¥100,000
022-02 Tama Dai ¥80,000
022-03 Tama Frames ¥18,000

01●素材／ファブリック・ニット・刺しゅう●サイズ／W900 D900 H350 ●カラー／ゴールド●限定1個
02●素材／ファブリック・ニット・ビーズ ●サイズ／W300 D300 H300 ●カラー／オリーブ・モス●セット内容／3個で1セット●限定各色1セット
03●素材／ファブリック・刺しゅう・ワイヤー●サイズ／W490 D20 H270 ●カラー／オレンジ・ブルー●受注制作限定10個

022-03

022-01/02
ニット、ビーズ、刺しゅう…黄金色のテーブルには多彩な色がちりばめられ、ゴージャス。イスのアクセントになっている渦巻き模様はところどころニットがフレームアウト。
This is a gorgeous golden-color table with various colors of wool, beads, and needle-work. A knitted whorl of wool is the accent for this chair.

写真多く入る部分はちょっと厚めのモノも入る網ポケット。網に小物やアクセサリーを掛けて飾ってもユニーク。
These photo frames have mesh-pockets inside, in which you can put thicker things. It will look good hanging on the wall with cute goods or accessories as a decoration.

テーブルの内側にセットされたライトを灯すと幻想的な姿が浮かび上がる。
Turn on the light inside the table to see something fantastic.

for people and also for fish **104**

023
JONATHAN E. AKERS

池や川がコンクリートで治水され、水草や魚、虫などの生息する水辺が減った今日。動植物の生態系、環境の回復を図る「ビオトープ」という考え方に基づく活動が世界的に進められている。自然と寄り添い暮らす豊かさ、心地よさ。そんな心の贅沢を日々の生活にも取り入れたい。

023-01・02/水草をモチーフにしたデコラティブ・ミラー。手鏡の01は把手をフックに掛けて壁かけにも。02は卓上用。どちらも把手が自由に曲がり、好みの角度に固定できる。

023-03/しなやかな曲線が優雅なテーブルは池をイメージ。表面はサンディング加工により、水面に広がる波紋や光の反射を連想させる。

These days, many aquatic plants, fish, and insects are losing their habitat because of flood-prevention works. Activities based on the idea called 'biotope', for the recovery of the ecosytems, environments, and habitats of animals and plants, is being promoted all over the world. It would be nice to be able to live our daily lives in a rich and comfortable communion with nature.
023-01・02/This is a decorative mirror with a water-plant motif. The hand-mirror, '01', can be used as a wall-mirror by hanging by its handle. '02' is a vanity or dresser-top mirror. Both have a flexible handle so you can adjust the angle. 023-03/This elegant table with graceful curves is made in the image of a pond. The surface has been sanded to create an impression of light reflecting off a ripple widening on the water.

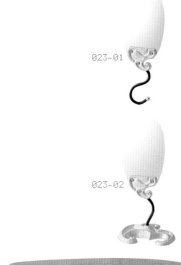

023-01

023-02

023-03

```
▌▌

WATER PLANET STORE
purchasing information P.136

023-01  Spud Mirror (Hand/Wall)
                        ¥15,000
023-02  Spud Mirror (Table)
                        ¥18,000
023-03  Pond Table      ¥20,000

01●素材／アルミ×ガラス ●サイズ／W160
H400 ●カラー／シルバー ●受注制作
02●素材／アルミ×ガラス ●サイズ／W160
D160 H400 ●カラー／シルバー ●受注制作
03●素材／アルミ ●サイズ／W620 D620 H370
●カラー／シルバー×ブルー ●受注制作

▌▌
```

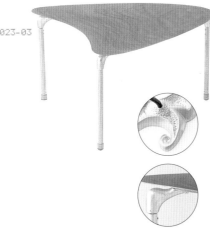

even on a rainy day

024   **SAKAI DESIGN ASSOCIATE**
-01/FOOD!

025   **HIDEO NAGAI**
-01/JUNGLE GYM FOR THE DOG
-02/BONE ACCESSORY SET

026   **DOG'N' DOG DAILY WEAR**
-01/RESCUE RAIN PARKA
-02/REVERSIBLE BANDANNA
-03/WATER PENDANT

What is that?

I was just wanting this!

It's only one...
025-01/JUNGLE GYM FOR THE DOG, 026-01/RESCUE RAIN PARKA, 03/WATER PENDANT

So I'm gonna find some food now.

024-01

ウラのキャップをはずして水を入れ、ウェイトを調整。
Remove the plug on the bottom and fill with water.
You can adjust the weight by the amount of water you add.

>>P134

SAKAI DESIGN ASSOCIATE

ミルク、ミネラルウォーター…。水モノを運ぶのは重くてツライ。誰もがマイナスに考えていたその"重さ"を、ポジティブに利用したウォーター・ダンベルの登場はとても画期的で、水の意外な利用法に気づかせてくれた。そしてその原理はまた、クリエーターにとって、新しい発想と可能性の源にもなっている。

024-01/"透明度のある安っぽい未来感"をテーマにデザインされた中・大型犬用エサ入れ。カラフルなシースルー容器は中が空洞になっていて、使用時に水を入れ重量を加える仕組み。満タンにすればビッグな愛犬がいくら激しく食べてもしっかり安定。しかも水を抜けば軽がる、持ち運びにもベンリなスグレモノ。

It is difficult and heavy work to carry liquids such as milk and mineral water. Everyone usually thinks of the weight of fluids in a negative way, so it is a very innovative invention which can use the heaviness of water in a positive way. The debut of the water dumbbell showed us an unexpected use of water, and its principle is the origin of new ideas and possibilities.

024-01/This is a food bowl for medium- to large-sized dogs, designed with a theme of "transparency and economical feeling for the future". This colorful clear container has a hollow interior in which you can put water to add heaviness when you feed your dog. It will be stable when your lovely big dog eats furiously! Also, it's light and easy to carry if you empty the water receptacle.

WATER PLANET STORE
purchasing information P.136

024-01 Food!   ¥5,000

01～03●素材／アクリル ●サイズ／W240 D170
H95 ●カラー／赤・青・黄（全てシースルー）

ただの飾り物でなく、もっと身近に、一般的に、人とアートがコミュニケーションできる機会を増やしたい。そんな彼の想いは、モノがあふれる現代社会で既製品にはない個性派作品を生み出している。

025-01/骨型ドッグフードを組み立てジャングルジムに。人間にとってコレは作品でも、犬にとっては単なる食べ物。一体犬がどういう反応をしめすのか…そんなユニークなたくらみが、犬と人とアートのコミュニケーションを楽しませてくれる。025-02/携帯ストラップ、チョーカー、キーホルダーの3点セットも骨型ドッグフードでドレスアップ。ストラップとチョーカーの革ヒモは黒と茶の2種類アリ。。

He wants to create more opportunities for people to communicate with art, not only for decorating, but so that they can feel closer to things. That's the reason his products are different from other things in this world filled with things.
025-01/A jungle gym assembled from bone-shaped dog biscuits. This is a work of art for people, but it's food for dogs. What would they do if they saw it? You will enjoy the communication between dogs, people, and art with this funny trick.
025-02/ A mobile-phone strap, a choker, and a key-ring are decorated with dog food. There are two color choices for the leather phone strap and choker: brown or black.

025-02
携帯電話ストラップ、キーホルダー
チョーカーの3点セット
A mobile-phone strap, a choker, and a key-ring, three of these articles make a set.

ドッグフードはすべて
樹脂コーティング済みのため、
食べられたり腐ったりする心配はナシ。
The dog food is completely coated with a resin, so you don't need to worry that is might be eaten or rot.

WATER PLANET STORE
purchasing information P.136

025-01 Jungle Gym For The Dog
                        ¥40,000
025-02 Bone Accessory Set
                         ¥4,500

01●素材／樹脂コーティング骨型ドッグフード ●サイズ／W500 D500 H550 ●カラー／ドッグフード色 ●受注制作
02●素材／樹脂コーティング骨型ドッグフード・革ヒモ・スチール ●サイズ／チョーカー:全長約380 携帯ストラップ:全長約200 キーホルダー:全長約105 ●カラー／黒×ドッグフード色・茶×ドッグフード色 ●受注制作

550
500 500

025-01

026
DOG' N' DOG DAILY WEAR

AM 5:00。撮影班集合。本日は犬ページの
ロケ日。主役はシーズーのハナ。2人の飼
い主に溺愛されている。AM 8:30。海岸到着。
空は快晴。真っ白な浜辺を駆け回るハナ。
追いかける撮影班。「待て」のカットを撮影
しようとするが命令には一向に従わないハナ。
エサでつるが効果ナシ。おいおい、頼むよ
ハナ。AM 10:00。骨をくわえるカット。ハナ
は骨が大好物。くわえて離さない。その骨は
お前には大きいよ。こらこら、だめだよ埋め
ちゃ。AM 11:00。どうやらハナは感づいた
ようだ。カメラマンの後ろに逃げると撮影が
中断することを。辛くなる度に後ろに回り込
むハナ。お前、こんな時は頭がいいね。PM
3:00。撮影終了。と、同時に急に元気にな
るハナ。お前、なぜその体力を撮影に活か
してくれないの。ともあれ、お疲れ様ハナ。
良い夢を。

The film crew assembled at 5:00AM. It was the dog's day on the set. The leading lady was Hana, a Shi-tzu who was doted upon by her two owners. We had an 8:30AM call on the beach. It was sunny, and Hana ran along the white-sand beach. The camera crew followed her. The script called for them to tape her obeying the command "STAY!", but Hana wasn't interested in obedience that day. They tried to bribe her with tasty treats, but it just didn't work.
"Oh, PLEEEASE, HANA!!!" 10:00AM; it's the take of Hana with a bone in her mouth. This is her favorite scene! She just won't let go! "It's too big for you! HEY! Don't bury it!" 11:00AM; Hana has figured-out that if she runs behind the cameraman, the director will yell, "CUT!", and filming will stop. So, when she gets tired, she tries to go behind the camera. Very clever! 3:00PM; We've wrapped for the day. Suddenly, Hana gets frisky! "You should have used that energy for the shoot, Hana! Oh, well... Thanks anyway... Sweet dreams, Hana!"

026-01

WATER PLANET STORE
purchasing information P.136

026-01
Rescue Rain Parka   ¥7,600
026-02 Reversible Bandanna
                 S,M ¥2,600
                 L,XL ¥3,200
026-03 Water Pendant ¥1,800

01●素材／表地:ナイロン100% 裏地:ナイロン
100% ●サイズ／S(背丈260,胴回り400) M(背丈
310,胴回り500) ●カラー／オレンジ ●限定60着
02●素材／綿100% ●サイズ／S:260 M:340
L:440 XL:540 ●柄／くじら柄×波柄・ハイビスカ
ス柄×光柄 ●限定100枚
03●素材／干草・ビーズ等 ●サイズ／S(220〜
320) M(320〜420) L(420〜540) ●カラー／ター
コイズブルー ●限定100個

首と胴のベルクロでサイズを調節。
トリコロールカラーのパイピングが小粋な
フードは、シーンに合わせて取り外し可能。
Hook and loop tape fasteners for the
neck and body make this easily
adjustable. The hood, with tri-color
piping, is removable.

026-02

026-03

くじら柄×波柄、
ハイビスカス柄×ストライプ柄の2タイプ。
There are two types:
- Whale and wave pattern.
- Hibiscus and stripe pattern.

バンダナにペンダントを
コーディネートすればさらにセンスアップ。
This pendant will go well with the bandana.

026-01/ナイロン素材をさらに強力にUPコーティングしたレインパーカーは、中が通気性バツグンのメッシュタイプだから、雨の日のお散歩もグンと快適。育ち盛りの愛犬も、サイズ調節できるからご安心を。背中にはおやつやおもちゃを入れておけるポケット付き。026-02/アウトドアのマストアイテム、バンダナはこだわり派ドッグも大満足のリバーシブル仕様。くじらバージョンは水を表現するブルーのグラデーション、ハイビスカスバージョンは太陽光線を表現するグラデーションで胸元をクールに演出。着けはずしもマジックテープでワンタッチ。026-03/ターコイズブルーの牛革をベースに、シルバーのアクセントを効かせた"水の花"ペンダント。サイズ調節もビーズをスライドするだけで簡単にジャストフィット。

026-01/ This coated nylon rain parka has a mesh lining to make it breathable so that walking on a rainy day is more comfortable. It's adjustable, so it's good for growing dogs. There's a pocket on the back where you can put dog-treats or toys.
026-02/ Necessities for outdoors people. Even fussy dogs will love this reversible bandana. The whale version has pattern of waves with blue gradation. The hibiscus version has a pattern of sunlight with gradation. They will look very attractive around your dog's neck. Hook and loop tape fasteners make it easy to put on and remove.
026-03/ A "water flower" pendant with an accent of silver on a base of turquoise-blue leather. A sliding bead makes the size easily adjustable.

海 洋 深 層 水

その不思議なチカラとは

Deep Sea Water　what is the wonderful power of this water?

海洋深層水とは、一般的には光合成に必要な太陽光が届かない水深200m以深で、水温が急に冷たくなっている層にある海水のことです。この太陽光が届かない深層の海で育まれた海洋深層水は、ミネラルバランスに優れ、栄養性に富んだ、とてもクリーンな水です。現在、取水地である高知県室戸市を拠点に、様々な分野で、その特性を活かすための研究が進められています。

Deep ocean water is sea water more than 200 meters deep, where the sunlight necessary for photosynthesis can't reach. The temperature of the water in this layer is dramatically colder than the water above. Water at these depths has a lot of minerals and rich nutrition. Now, a study is being promoted by Muroto City, in Kochi Prefecture, on how to exploit the features of the lower depths in various ways.

low-temperature stability
低温安定性

nutrition content
富栄養性

清浄性
degree of purity

海洋深層水の特性
The special quality of
deep sea water

age of the water
熟成性

ミネラル特性
the mineral content

SEAWa

Deep

ter

Use for beauty and medicine

皮膚細胞を、適度なミネラルで
優しく包み込みます。

It covers skin cells with moderate amounts of minerals.

室戸沖の海洋深層水は、地球規模で大循環する深層水の湧昇流を水深320m以深の取水口から採取した水です。
陸水由来の大腸菌や一般細菌をはじめ、陸や大気からの化学物質に汚染されておらず、海洋性細菌数も表層海水に
比べて少ないクリーンな海水です。また、様々なミネラルがバランス良く含まれているのも大きな特徴です。これらの特
性をもつ海洋深層水は人間の皮膚にとても優しく、美容や医療といった分野で、化粧品や入浴剤などの商品に活用
されており、とくに医療分野では、アトピー性皮膚炎への効果が期待されています。

The deep ocean water off the coast of Muroto City is from a large column of rising water at a depth of 320 meters. It is not
contaminated with colon bacilli or any other bacteria or chemical substances from the land or the air,
and also has less ocean bacteria compared with surface ocean water. One important feature is its ideal balance of a variety
of minerals. Deep ocean water is good for our skin. It's used for cosmetics and bath powder in the cosmetics industry, and in
the field of medicine, it's expected to be effective in the treatment of atopic dermatitis.

海洋深層水は、その特性を活かして様々な食品が開発されています。たとえば、海洋深層水を使った食塩は、深層水に含まれたにがり成分により、味がまろやかになります。また、醤油や味噌、清酒など醸造によりできる食品は、そのにがり成分により発酵が促進されるといわれています。とくに清酒醸造の場合には、適度な量を用いると、アルコール収得率が増し、アミノ酸度が低く吟醸香の多い、品質の高い清酒ができます。また、クリーンでミネラルバランスの良い海洋深層水は、清涼飲料水にも用いられ、現在もさらに多くの食品開発が進められています。

味をまろやかにし、発酵を
促進させるチカラがあります。
It makes flavor milder and can accelerate fermentation.

#02

Use in the food industry

Various foods are developed from deep ocean water products. For example, salt from deep ocean water makes the flavor of food milder by the action of bittern, which is present in the water. Bittern also accelerates the fermentation of foods which are brewed by a fermentation process, like soy sauce, miso (soybean paste), and sake. Especially for sake brewing, bittern increases the alcohol content, lowers the amino acid content, and helps produce a delicious bouquet of high-quality sake. Bittern is also good for the production of soft drinks.

The architect's concept

交流ゾーン
Communicator zone

企業ゾーン
Business zone

インキュベーターゾーン
Incubator zone

取水地、高知県室戸市には、
「MUROTO DEEP SEA WORLD」の建設が進んでいます。

"Muroto Deep-Sea World" is now
under construction in Muroto City, Kochi Prefecture,
where "the deep ocean water" can be collected.

❶ 海洋深層水取水・給水ターミナル
❷ オープンラボラトリー
❸ 商業施設
❹ タラソテラピー
❺ ホテル
❻ 海洋深層水プール

❶ Terminal for deep ocean water collection and supply.
❷ Open laboratory
❸ Business facility
❹ Thalassotherapy
❺ Hotel
❻ Swimming pool containing deep ocean water

高知県では、1998年に科学技術庁の地域先導研究を導入し、国や県の研究機関、大学、民間企業等の頭脳や最先端技術を結集して、海洋深層水の新たな特性の究明を始めました。また、取水地である高知県室戸市には「ムロト・ディープ・シー・ワールド」が計画され、ここを海洋深層 水研究とビジネスの拠点として、健康・医療やバイオテクノロジー、エネルギーなど幅広い分野で の高度利用を目指した計画が 進められています。

In Kochi Prefecture, in 1998, the Science and Technology Agency has assembled a think-tank made up of top academic and industry experts to study the benefits of deep ocean water. They are planning to build a facility called "Muroto Deep-Sea World" in Muroto City. It will be a center for deep ocean research and industries, which aim to exploit deep ocean water for health, medicine, bio-technology, and energy.

DEEP SEA WATER POSTER GRANDPRIX -2000

「海洋深層水」をテーマに、ポスター作品を募集します。

An invitation for entries for posters to publicize "the deep ocean water".

「WATER PLANET」では、「海洋深層水」を広くPRするポスター作品を募集いたします。深海に広がる世界のイメージやクリーンでミネラルバランスに富んだ特性など、切り口は自由。未知の可能性を秘めた「海洋深層水」を読者の方々の独自の視点と感性で表現してください。

WATER PLANET is inviting entries for posters to publicize "the deep ocean water". Please express all the unknown possibilities of "the deep ocean water" with originality and feeling. What you express is up to you, such as the image of the deep-sea world, or its clean and mineral-rich qualities. We expect great posters which can show the image of the deep ocean water to the public.

<出品募集内容>
■テーマ／海洋深層水 ■サイズ／B1・タテ型 ■表現方法／自由。(ただし平面作品に限る)
■審査・賞／東京アートディレクターズクラブに所属するクリエイター諸氏により審査し、各賞を選出。
　最優秀グランプリ賞 1名 (表彰状と賞金)／準グランプリ賞 2名 (表彰状と賞金)
■応募締め切り／平成12年5月10日
■発表／本誌3号の誌面にて、受賞作品と作者を紹介いたします。

< Call for Entries>
■Theme／Deep Sea Water. ■Size／B-1size. ■Method／Any two-dimensional medium will be accepted.
■Judgement and Award／The poster contest will be judged by members of the Tokyo Art Directors' Club. One Grand Prize winner will be declared and presented with a certificate of commendation and prize money. Second Prize: two winners will receive a certificate of commendation and prize-money.
■Deadline for entries／Must be received by: Wednesday, May 10, 2000, Japan Standard Time
■Announcement／The winner will be announced in the third issue of WATER PLANET with pictures of the winning entry and the artist. We are also planning to exhibit the Grand Prix winner at other promotional events.

※詳しい情報については、P.138の募集要項を参照して下さい。

ゴッホなら、見抜けるかも知れない。

人類のために、進化した水。

医療用電解水生成器
ヒューマンウォーター
＜HU-50＞

医療用具承認番号 20900BZZ00897000
標準小売価格 186,000円 (税別)
交換用浄水カードリッジ 12,000円 (税別)

株式会社 OSGコーポレーション　本社 〒530-0043 大阪市北区天満1丁目26番3号 (OSG本社ビル) TEL: 06-6357-0101 (代表)　東京営業本部 〒154-0003 東京都世田谷区野沢2丁目1番4号 (OSG東京営業本部ビル) TEL: 03-3795-8371 (代表)

OSG
http://www.osg-nandemonet.co.jp/

EAST&WEST
Hideaki Matsumoto

Products Designer

Profile

'64年、神奈川県生まれ。'87年に東京造形大学を卒業後、（株）イノウエインダストリィズ入社。'90年にアジア・ヨーロッパ遊学した後、'91年にEAST&WESTを設立。家具インテリアデザインを中心に活動。

He was born in Kanagawa Prefecture in 1964. After he graduated from Tokyo Zokei University, he started working for Inoue Industries Co., Inc. He went to Asian and European countries in 1990. After that, he established EAST & WEST in 1991. Now, his main work is furniture and interior design.

Message

僕のデザインを見た人が、「エッ!何だこれは?」「そうか、こういうものなんだ!」「よし使ってみよう!」と思うような物づくりを目指しています。

I expect people who see my products to say "What is it?', "It's easy! Let's try it!".

| #000 | P022 | JPN | tel:03-5368-6469　03-5368-6479
e-mail:furnitur@bekkoame.ne.jp |

Yoshihiko Mamiya

Interior Designer

Profile

大阪生まれ。インテリアデザイナー、株式会社インフィクス代表。「CLUB ASIA」「UN CAFE」「GRAND CAFE」「ZEPP OSAKA」など、東京・大阪を中心に話題のスペースを次々と手掛け、'98年には自身の作品を作品集「spaces and projects infix」に集約。

He was born in Osaka. He is an interior designer and a representative director of Infix Co., Inc. He has designed many popular places in Osaka and Tokyo, such as 'Club Asia', 'Un Cafe', 'Grand Cafe', and 'Zepp Osaka'. He published 'spaces and projects infix', a collection of his work, in 1998.

Message

ミュージアムに飾られたアートを眺めるのも楽しいが、創造的なフォルムと一緒に暮らし、身近に使いながら感じてみたら、さらに楽しい。家具と人の関係を、ちょっと新しいカタチで楽しんでみてほしい。

Although it's nice to look at art in the museum, it is even nicer to live with creative forms and feel them. I want people to enjoy the relationship between furniture and humans in a different way.

| #001 | P022 | JPN | e-mail:mamiya-infix@ma.neweb.ne.jp |

Naoko Hirota

Bag Designer

Profile

東京生まれ。'90年、東京芸術大学卒業、'96年、廣田デザインスタジオ設立。国際バッグデザイン豊岡94（金賞）、米国IDMagazine Design Review'98（Honorable Mention賞）、デザインフォーラム'99（金賞）。

She was born in Tokyo, and graduated from Tokyo National University of Fine Arts & Music in 1990. She then established Hirota Designing Studio. She was awarded the gold medal at the International Bag Design in Toyooka in 1994. In 1998, she was received Honorable Mention in the ID Magazine Design Review in the U.S.A, and she was awarded the gold medal at the Design Forum in 1999.

Message

nAocAのバッグのデザインコンセプトは「手に持つ器」です。バッグである前に手に持つ器としてどんなものが気持ちいいんだろうということから物づくりを始めます。そうすることで、既成概念にとらわれない新しいものが生まれると考えるからです。

The concept of nAocA's bags is "The container in a hand". I think, "What kind of container would be easy to hold?" when I start making things. I believe that if I keep this thought in mind, I won't make a

| #002 | P023 | JPN | tel:03-3423-7105　fax:03-3423-7014
e-mail:hirota1@alles.or.jp |

宿野輪天堂
Shukuno-Rintendo
Hiroaki Okada

Bicycle Designer

Profile

'65年大阪府生まれ。'94年に「宿野輪天堂」を設立。以来、通常の自転車屋としての業務の傍ら「乗って、見て、楽しい」ことをテーマに、心に訴える愉快な自転車を企画・製作している。

He was born in Osaka in 1965. He established 'Shukuno Rintendo' in 1994. In addition to his regular bicycle shop business, he designs and produces funny bikes which appeal to people's feelings under the theme of 'Enjoy riding and making'.

Message

最近は、次世代の自転車「リカンベント」の開放的でゆったりと時間の流れる乗り味に、心を奪われています。

Recently, I've been fascinated with the next-generation bike 'Recumbent', which is frank and makes time go slower when I'm riding it.

| #003 | P024 | JPN | tel:0727-34-2694　fax:0727-34-2694
e-mail:mail@rintendo.com　http://www.rintendo.com |

GENKOTU
Toru Tatizawa
Ichigo Sugawara

Design Unit

Profile

"GENKOTU"は創造するコミュニティとして、'99に スタートした。写真家の菅原一剛とデザイナーでパン ザイペイント主宰の立沢トオルのコラボレーションでは、 実生活から多くの"創造の種"を得ながら活動している。

GENKOTU began as a creative community in 1999. It's a collaborarion between photographer Ichigo Sugawara, and Toru Tachizawa, a designer and director of 'Bonzai Paint'. Their activity get a lot of 'Seeds of Creation' from everyday life.

Message

ここにミネラルウォーターの空きボトルがあって、僕た ちはそれを潰した。潰れたボトルはどれ一つとして同じ ものはなく、僕のようにも、君のようにも見えた。あるも のは年齢すら感じさせた。僕たちは潰れたボトルを記 録することだけに注意した。

Here are some empty mineral water bottles, and we have squashed them. None of them look the same. Some look like me, and others look like you. Some of them even show their age. We just concentrated on making a record of squashed PET bottles.

| #004 | P025 | JPN | e-mail:toru-t@tka.att.ne.jp |

Paul Daly

Interior Designer

Profile

ロンドンのHOXTON SQUREIに活動基盤を置くポール・ デイリーデザインスタジオは、様々な分野のコンテンポ ラリーなデザインの日用品を取り扱っている。伝統的な 材料や現代的な材料を用い、家庭用や商業用の家具の コンセプト開発から制作までを行っている。

Paul Daly Design Studio deals with a wide variety of contemporary design needs from its base in Hoxton Square, London. The studio develops both domestic and commercial furniture in traditional + contemporary materials from concept to production.

Message

キューバの水は波打って、塩辛かった。私がフローテー ションタンクの中で過ごした時間は3時間。水は、肌の 乾燥など実に色々な問題を解決してくれる。まるで、パ ブがそうしてくれるようにね…。

The water in Cuba was wavy and salty. My time spent in a flotation tank has been 3 hours. Water can really solve any problem about dry skin and so on. Pubs can do the same.

| #005 | P025 | IRL | tel:03-5485-8461
e-mail:info@eandy.com (E&Y co., Ltd) |

Nobuhiko Suzuki

Artist

Profile

'69年、神奈川県に生まれる。'95年～'97年、渡伯。帰 国後、'98年、ブンカムラギャラリー(東京)、'99年には、 NICAF99・ギャラリー椿(東京)で個展を開催。

He was born in Kanagawa Prefecture in 1969. He lived in Brazil from 1995 to 1997. After his return, he had exhibitions at 'Bunkamura Gallery' in Tokyo in 1998, and 'Gallery Tsubaki's booth at NICAF '99 in Tokyo in 1999.

Message

'00年4月中旬より京都大雅堂、6月には東京ブンカム ラギャラリーで個展を開催。また、1月～2月にはワコー ル銀座アートスペース、京都マロニエのグループ展に 参加。3月にはソウルのアートフェアにも出展します。 美術にこだわらず幅広い活動を予定しています。

I will have an exhibition at Taigado in Kyoto in the middle of April, and at Bunkamura Gallery in Tokyo in June. I will join the group exhibition at Wacoal Ginza Art Space and at marronnier in Kyoto in January and Februrary. My work will be exhibited at Art Fair in Seoul in March. I'm planning a variety of artistic activities in a variety of media.

| #006 | P029 | JPN | |

Shinichiro Arakawa

Fashion Designer

Profile

'89年に渡仏。パリの服飾学校ベルソーを卒業後、'93 年に初めてパリコレクションに参加。'95年には、東京下 北沢でのストリートショーで東京コレクション初参加。 以降HONDAとのコラボレーションショー等、コレクショ ン発表では、常に話題を投げかける。

He went to France in 1989, and he graduated from Berceau, the fashion design school in Paris. His first entry to the Paris Collection was in 1993. He joined the Tokyo Collection at the street show in Shimokitagawa, Tokyo, in 1995. He collaborates with Honda, and his new collection releases are always headline news.

Message

水の中を自由に泳ぐ魚のような、服づくりをしたい。

I'd like to make clothes as freely as a fish swimming in the water.

| #007 | P031 | JPN | tel:03-5778-2199 fax:03-3486-1725
e-mail:sa8133@mu2.so-net.ne.jp http://www.0cm4.co.jp |

this is it.
Beth Howthorn
Robert Studer

Products Designers

Profile

ベスとロバートは'95年に出会い、現在はカナダのバンクーバーで制作活動を続けている。彼らは95%の時間を夫婦として二人一緒に過ごしているが、普遍の芸術性を追求することで得られる、世界中の素晴らしい人達との出会いを、とても大切にしている。

Beth and Robert met in 1995. Now they work together in Vancouver, Canada. They spend 95% of their time together as a married couple. Their search for timeless simplicity in their work and lives has allowed them to meet many wonderful people around the world.

Message

どんなことでも、気持ちを込めてすればうまくいくものです。そしてあなたが仕事を楽しいと感じ、私たちの作品に喜びを見いだしてくれれば、光栄です。 ～水をたくさん飲んでくださいね！～

It doesn't matter what you do, as long as it is done with your heart. Things will flow and you will be cared for. Our only hope is that you find joy in what you do and pleasure in the things we make. And remember to drink lots of water.

| #008 | P034 | CAN | tel:03-3437-3331　fax:03-3437-3325 e-mail:devise@adcore.co.jp （AD CORE DEVISE INC.） |

Junzo Kuroda

Artist

Profile

'68年生まれ。武蔵野美術大学建築学科、東京工業大学坂本一成研究室を経て、'96年よりフリーで建築家・芸術家活動を開始。作品に「桃色の運椅子」「Washman」「ソフトハウス」など。都市サーベイ「メイド・イン・トーキョー」も共同展開中。

He was born in 1968. He has been a freelane architect and artist since 1996, after studying at the architecture department of Musashino Art University and the studio of Sakamoto Issei at Tokyo Industrial University. His main works are "Momoiro no Neisu" (Pink Couch), "Washman", and "Soft House". Now he is writing a city survey called "Made in Tokyo" in collaboration with others.

Message

2000年に、「メイド・イン・トーキョー」を共著にて出版予定。2000年以降も、春―夏―秋―冬、雑貨、インテリア、建築、環境、都市、現代美術を "think different" で "just do it" で go! go! go! 。

I'm planning to publish "Made in Tokyo", with some other people in 2000. After 2000, in every season, I'll be thinking about products, interior design, architecture, the environment, cities, and modern art, and I want to "think different" and "just do it!".

| #009 | P063 | JPN | http://www.iloveshops.com　e-mail:junzo@rb3.so-net.ne.jp http://www.dnp.co.jp/museum/nmp/madeintokyo/mit.html |

あぐら家具企画
Furniture Design AGRA

Furniture Designer

Profile

東京生まれ。武蔵野美術大学卒業後、北海道旭川市の家具メーカーにて工場勤務。'95年「あぐら家具企画」(旭川市)を設立。家具ライブ、企画展多数と幅広い活動を展開。オリジナル家具のデザインから、製作、販売まで を行っている。

She was born in Tokyo. After graduating from Musashino Art University, she worked for a furniture company's factory in Asahikawa City in Hokkaido. She established Furniture Design Agra in 1995 in Asahikawa. She's very active designing furniture and planning exhibiions. Furniture Design Agra does furniture design, production, and sales.

Message

あぐら家具企画では、「クールな大人のキュートな生活」を提案すべく、"いとおしくて気持ちのいい家具" を作り続けています。カタログによる通信販売も行っておりますので、ご注文の際には、カタログも併せてご請求ください。

Furniture Design Agra keeps producing lovely and comfortable furniture to provide "cute life for cool adults". We have a catalog of our products. Please ask for a copy when you order.

| #010 | P064 | JPN | tel:0166-34-0898　fax:0166-34-0928　e-mail:agra@meme.co.jp http://city.hokkai.or.jp/~agra/plofile/plofile.html |

SOUP DESIGN
Nobuaki Doi
Satoshi Watanabe
Yayoi Yamashiro
Rie Kuroiwa
Fumikazu Ohara

Design Unit

Profile

建築、料理、インテリア、グラフィックなど、異ジャンルの5人で結成。'99年に、happening '99、E&Y主催のEX-tensionに参加。現在PP（ポリプロピレン）を用いた什器のデザインを進行中。

It's a collaboration of five people from different fields; architecture, cooking, interior and graphic design. In 1999, they joined "Happening '99" and Extension, sponsored by E&Y. Now, they are designing polypropylene utensils.

Message

- - -

- - -

| #011 | P064 | JPN | e-mail:soup@01.246.ne.jp http://www.d2.dion.ne.jp/~ohara34/soup/ |

love the life
Akemi Katsuno
Takashi Yagi

Interior Design Unit

Profile

ラヴザライフは勝野明美とヤギタカシのデザインオフィス。店舗・住宅の内外装を中心に、建築、グラフィックまでを含めて空間に関わるデザイン全般を手掛けている。ラヴザライフとそのプロダクトレーベル、勝野屋へのコンタクトは下記まで。

Love the Life is the design office of Akemi Katsuno and Takashi Yagi. They produce interior and exterior graphic and architectural detailing for shops and dwellings. The following is the contact address of Love the Life and their product label, Katsunoya.

Message

勝野屋はニホンのホームプロダクトを取り巻く現状をドキュメントするアートプロジェクトです。制作の過程で起こったことや私たちが感じたことをホームページでご覧いただけます。今回の掲載作品から、2001年へかけてラインナップを完成させていきます。

Katsunoya is the art project which documents a state of home products in Japan. We'll show you the production process and what we felt on our homepage. We will compile a catalog of our products from the ones in this magazine in 2000-2001.

#012	P082	JPN

tel:03-3723-6267 fax:03-3723-6267
e-mail:info@lovethelife.org e-mail:info@katsunoya.com
http://lovethelife.org http://www.katsunoya.com

Patrick Rimond

Photographer

Profile

来日して3年。その間に撮った写真により、大阪、京都、パリで個展を開催。日本と自分自身について学んだことを表現した写真作品に、最近では多くのファンができつつある。

It has been three years since he came to Japan. He has had exhibitions in Osaka, Kyoto, and Paris of his photographs from the last three years. His photographs, which express the things he has learned about Japan and himself, are becoming increasingly popular.

Message

朝の葉の上に、ひとしずくの水。私は水であり、水は地球。水は日々、私の肌を流れ落ち、母の子宮の中で、私は泳ぐ。私の体内あるいは海の中で水は波紋を作るように私を優しく包んでくれる。

A drop of water on a morning leaf, I'm water, water is earth. Water runs on my skin. Everyday in my mother's belly. I swam in my body or in the sea water goes as a circle water cares about me so do I.

#013	P083	FRA

e-mail:patrickrimond@hotmail.com

Benoa Berger

Illustrator

Profile

'75年パリ生まれ。'95年、Sorbone Universityにて美術を専攻。パリの「Nova Magazine Contest」においてイラストで初受賞。'99年よりベルリンの雑誌「NEID BEITRAG」でイラストを描く。'99年来日。

He was born in Paris in 1975. His major at Sorbonne University was art. His illustration was awarded in the Nova Magazine Contest in 1999. He has been drawing in 'NEID BEITRAG' in Berlin since 1999. He visited Japan in 1998.

Message

この本が発売される頃には、パリで2つめのポストカードコレクションの準備をしながら、新しいプロジェクトに携わっているのではないかと思います。(1つめのポストカードコレクションは大阪の「ACKNE Design Books Store」で販売中)

When this catalog will be come out, I will be preparing my second postcards collection in Paris working with CROSS. The first one is selling at the ACKNE Design Books Store in Osaka. And certainly I will be engaging in new creative projects.

#014	P083	FRA

e-mail:bbenoa@yahoo.com

Takao Yamashita
beauty:beast

Fashion Designer

Profile

'66年、長崎市生まれ。土木建築学科出身。'91年、S/S大阪コレクションでデビュー。'94・95年、A/Wコレクションでパリコレクションデビュー。翌年より東京コレクションに参加。

He was born in Nagasaki in 1966, and graduated from the civil engineering and architecture department of university. His Osaka Collection debut was the Spring/Summer Collection in 1991. His Paris Collection debut was the 1994 and 1995 Autumn/Winter Collection. He joined the Tokyo Collection in 1996.

Message

それは、とても柔軟で、色を含め変形自在なトランスフォーマー。自然のエレメントの中でも多大な力を持つピュアな存在。十分な環境適応性を持つが故に無駄なものも無く、あらゆるシステムに自在に侵入し、共存することも可能なもの。その特性を思考に置換えた時それはsubconsciousness。

It is the transformer which is flexible and free to change its color and shape. Its existence is pure and it is one of the most powerful forces of elements of nature. It is environmentally adaptable, so it's efficient, and it is able to enter other systems and survive. If you could think of one word to describe it, it would be "subconsciousness".

#015	P084	JPN

tel:03-5468-5444 fax:03-5467-0914
http://www.beautybeast.co.jp

"graf"
**decorative mode no.3
design products
Shigeki Hattori**

Industrial Design Unit

Profile

'93年、UNIT結成。「少年探偵団」をテーマにあらゆるジャンルの6人が集結。照明の展覧会など、ライフスタイルすべての空間を共に提案してきた。'97年4月,大阪ショールームである"graf"をオープンし現在に至る。

Established UNIT in 1993. Brought six people together from various fields under the theme "Youth Detective Squad." The group held an exhibition based around lighting and created multiple spaces for all lifestyles. In April 1997, it opened the Osaka showroom "graf," which is still active today.

Message

2000年3月13日～東京品川のコクヨショールームにて、我々の展覧会を開催します。同時に作品集的プロモーションビデオを発売予定。乞う期待!!

We will hold an exhibition at the Kokuyo showroom in Tokyo's Shinagawa on March 13, 2000. We'll also be selling a promotional video of our works to date. See you there!!

#016	P084	JPN

tel:06-6543-1819   fax:06-6543-1819
e-mail:shige-d3@ra2.so-net.ne.jp

Hiroyuki Nakano

Moving Image Creator

Profile

映像作家。音楽的映像と宇宙的自然の映像、そして映画を創作中。「SFサムライ・フィクション」に続く「SFステレオ・フューチャー」の制作中。また、屋久島の水を世界一愛するマニア。小笠原のイルカ「ピースブルー」のロングバージョンは、水マニア必見。

Moving Image Creator. Now, he is making musical images, spacial images, and a film, which is called "SF Stereo Future", the sequel to "SF Samurai Fiction". He is an enthusiast of water in Yakushima. Water buffs shouldn't miss the long version of "Peace Blue" about dolphins in Ogasawara.

Message

人にとって水と酸素が一番大切。そんな想いで、新作の映画も制作しています。屋久島に行く度に、心を奪われるのが「透明な水」。30時間以上ある素材を個人的に編集した、心和むビデオをおすそ分けしたいと思います。自然に創り出す動きは、最高のアートです。

Water and oxygen are the most important things for humans. I'm making a new film with this feeling. I'm attracted to "pure water" every time I go to Yakushima. The original film is more than 30 hours long. I shortened it for myself. I'd like to share this video with other people. The movement that nature creates is the best art.

#017	P085	JPN

tel:03-5721-8288 fax:03-5721-8287 e-mail:peace@peacedelic.co.jp
http://www.peacedelic.co.jp/nakano/

SILICON baby

Accessories Designer

Profile

'69年京都生まれ。'93年、京都市立芸術大学美術学部美術学科卒業。'95年、京都市立芸術大学美術研究科彫刻専攻修了。'95年"SILICON baby"ジュエリースタジオを設立。

Born in Kyoto in 1969. Graduated in 1993 from the Fine Arts Department of Kyoto City University of Arts. Completed further studies specializing in sculpture in 1995. Established the "SILICON baby" jewelry studio in 1995.

Message

私たち人間は有機生命体であり、この地球上では水なくしては立つことも、歩くことも、会話することも、ましてモノを創ることもできないでしょう。全ての生き物にとって、水のない世界=死なのです。私もあなたも毎日数十キロの水を担ぎ世界を旅するのです。

Human beings are living organisms that depend on water for everything. Without water we could not stand, walk, or talk, much less create things on the Earth. To all living beings, the absence of water means death. Both you and I carry a few dozen kilograms of water around the Earth every day.

#018	P091	JPN

tel:075-762-2335   fax:075-762-2335
e-mail:space007@mbox.kyoto-inet.or.jp

Photo by Taro Mizunuma

EXIT
metal work supply

Products Design Unit

Profile

商業空間、店舗デザイン設計を中心に、家具やプロダクト等の製作までを行うデザインカンパニー。東京を中心に活動中。

A design company focusing on commercial spaces and store design as well as making furniture and products. Mainly active in the Tokyo area.

Message

スケルトンの奥にある望みって、もしかしたら水の存在を欲しているって事なのかな?「最近渇いているのかな?」

Skeleton design perhaps holds within it people's longing for water in life. "Has it been dry recently?"

#019	P102	JPN

e-mail:exit@exit-mws.co.jp

D.R.T,
Zoe Cappon
Jonathan Delachaux

Artists

Profile

2人は、スイスのアーティスト。'98年に結婚し、D.R.T, というグループ名で仕事をしている。D.R.Tの主な仕事は、裸のアーティストをテーマにした絵画やパフォーマンス、ビデオアート、写真等。'98年以来、ヨーロッパや日本の展覧会にも多数参加している。

They are Swiss artists. They got married in 1998 and decided to work together as D.R.T. Their work consists mostly of painting, performance, video art, and graphics. They have taken part in many exhibitions in Europe and Japan since 1998. Their main subject is naked artists.

Message

2年前から、「仕事場にいる裸のアーティスト」（ビデオ）コレクションのために、私たちは裸を撮影させてもらえないかと、多くのアーティストを訪ねました。彼らの多くは同意してくれ、カメラの前で数々のアートパフォーマンスを見せてくれたんです。これを読んで興味をもったアーティストの方々、連絡をお待ちしています。

For the last two years, we have been asking artists to let us film them in the nude in their work-place. Many artists have agreed and have done some kind of art performance nude in front of our video camera. If you are interested in taking part in this type of project, please contact:

#020 | P102 | CHE   e-mail:drt00@hotmail.com

Hiroko Hosomi

Accessories Designer

Profile

'67年大阪生まれ。'90年にコスチューム・ジュエリーブランド "バンブー・マジック" 設立。'97年より個展活動をはじめ、よりアーティスティックなオブジェやアクセサリーを展開する。

She was born in Osaka in 1967. She established "BAMBOO MAGIC", a costume and jewelry brand in 1990. She has begun to have her own exhibitions and has created even more artistic objects and accessories.

Message

深海に住む生き物をはじめ、自然界における生き物たちがインスピレーションのモト。「頑張れ！」とか話しかけながら作品を創っています。植物も語りかけながら育てるほうがいいっていうし、知らない間に勝手に動き出しそうな私の作品には "気" が入っているのかも。

The source of my inspiration is deep sea creatures and the natural world. I say "You can do it!" to my products while I'm making them. People say that it is good to speak to your plants. My products, which seem to start moving by themselves, might have their own spirits.

#021 | P103 | JPN   tel:072-863-6611   fax:072-863-6611
e-mail:h727@osk2.3web.ne.jp

---

atelier SU:SO
Kaori Umeda
Yukiko Uno

Artists

Profile

それぞれが創作活動を行う傍ら、'95年にファイバーアートのユニット "atlier SU:SO" を結成。'96年、'97年にgalery T.K.artにて作品展を開催。

Atelier SU:SO, which is a fiber art collaboration, was organized in1995 by the artists, who continued to do their own, individual works at the same time. They had exhibitions at the "Gallery T.K. Art" in 1996 and 1997.

Message

いろいろな "場" から、様々な波動が、それぞれの目的を持って行き交っていることを感じると、目に見えない情報に敏感でいたいと思う。"エネルギー" や "めぐり" を大切にした物づくりをしていきたい。

We want to be sensitive to the invisible information we get from the emanations we feel from things all around us. We think a great deal about energy and fortune when we create things.

#022 | P104 | JPN

AXY design group
Jonathan E. Akers

Furniture Designer

Profile

'64年、NY生まれ。'87年、NY Metal Maniaにてラルフローレン・ノールインターナショナル等の家具を制作。'92年、来日。兵庫県尼崎市の町工場で、AXY design groupを設立。

He was born in New York in 1964. He produced furniture for Ralph Lauren and Knoll International at NY Metal Mania. He established "AXY Design Group" in the factory in Amagasaki City, Hyogo Prefecture, in Japan in 1992.

Message

私の夢は、誰もが毎日使うモノで、実用的でありながら好奇心くすぐるようなモノを創造すること。つまり、アートと実用性の優れたバランスを表現すること。

I dream of creating interesting and functional objects, to be use in everyone's daily living. A strong balance between art and function.

#023 | P105 | USA   tel:06-4704-3052   fax:06-4704-3052
e-mail:spaceaxy@gol.com

SAKAI DESIGN ASSOCIATE
Toshihiko Sakai

Products Designer

Profile

'64年高知県生まれ。'87年に東京造形大学を卒業後、'92年に(有)サカイデザインアソシエイツを設立。コンピュータ周辺機器、家電製品のデザインの傍ら、家具のデザインも手掛ける。

Born in Kochi Prefecture in 1964. Graduated Tokyo University of Art and Design in 1987 and established Sakai Design Associates in 1992. Designs furniture in addition to designing computer peripherals and home electrical appliances.

Message

海は好きですが、今回のデザインでは水は特に意識したものではなく"重さ"のために必要だったからです。ただ、えさ入れの中に封入された水を見ていると、"重さ以上"のものを感じるような気がします。

I like the sea, but for this design I did not think much about water because I was looking for "heaviness." But looking at the water in the feeder, it feels more than heavy.

| #024 | P114 | JPN | tel:03-5363-1039 fax:03-5363-1038
e-mail:sakai@sakaidesign.com http://www.sakaidesign.com

Hideo Nagai

Artist

Profile

'88年〜'91年、アカデミー・グランショミエール(フランス)、アート・スチューデント・リーグ オブ ニューヨーク。'90年、バルセロナ展・SALA DE ARTE CANUDA(スペイン)'99年、ギャラリー白(大阪)で個展。以降'99年まで毎年、大阪を中心に個展を開催。

Studied at Acadamie Grande Chaumiere in France and at the Art Student League of New York from 1988-1991. In 1990, He participated in the Barcelona exhibition, Sala de Arte Canuda and he had exhibitions at 'Gallery Shiro' in Osaka in 1999, Held individual exhibitions every year up until 1999, primarily in Osaka.

Message

日常生活ではアートと接する機会は少ないと思われます。が、アートと接することで日常生活では得られない新しい体験ができると思います。私は既製品にはない楽しい体験ができる作品づくりを通して、アートとコミュニケーションする機会を増やしたいと考えます。

For people who say they have little chance to see art in their everyday lives, I would say art can be a new experience that one cannot get in daily life. By making art to provide a pleasurable experience found in no other ready-made products, I want people to have more opportunity to experience art and communication.

| #025 | P115 | JPN | tel:0725-21-0701 fax:0725-21-0701

**DOG'N'DOG
DAILY WEAR**
Chikako Hosoi
Eiko Fujii

Fashion Designers

Profile

'98年、東京を中心にDOG' N' DOGブランドをスタート。'99年、オフィスを関西に移し、代官山、渋谷、横浜、大阪、神戸などの雑貨店やペットグッズショップを中心に商品展開。2000年に向けてN.Y.でも商品展開をスタート。

The Dog 'N' Dog brand was launched in Tokyo in 1998. In 1999, the office moved to the Kansai area, developing products primarily for pet goods shops in Daikanyama, Shibuya, Yokohama, Osaka, and Kobe. In 2000, its goal is to develop products to sell in New York.

Message

「この服ならぜひ着せてみたい」と思えるような、単純な可愛さにこだわって作っていきたい。ギャル大阪(スプール)では、いろいろな商品を展開中。ぜひ、足を運んでみて!!

I want to make clothes with a simple adorableness that makes one think "I want my pet to wear that!" I am in the process of developing various products at Galley Osaka (Spool). Come and visit!

| #026 | P116 | JPN | tel:0792-83-5538 fax:0792-83-5538

Ken Hamazaki

Artist

Profile

'67年生まれ。'87年、渡英。帰国後、「迷宮(迷路)」と「包む」をテーマにアート活動を開始。'92年、自らのギャラリー"KEN HAMAZAKI ART COLLECTION"をオープン(後移転)。'97年、自らの美術館"浜崎健立現代美術館"を開館。

Born in 1967. Went to England in 1987. After returning to Japan, began working in art with the themes of "labyrinths" and "enclosure." Opened his own gallery in 1992, the Ken Hamazaki Art Collection (which has since moved). In 1997, he opened his own art museum, the Ken Hamazaki Museum of Modern Art.

Message

ボクはなぜか週末になると水をよく飲みます。1日、10リットル飲みます。水はおいしいです。なぜか週末になると水にとりつかれます。だから、この本に参加してアメリカの砂漠でお茶会をして、世界中の人に会いました。ボクは思いました。日本って面白いなぁ?そう一瞬で「水」を「氷」にしてしまう人種。おわり。

Why is it that I drink lots of water on weekends? I can drink 10 liters in a day. I love water. Why is it that I become obsessed with water on weekends? That's why I am participating in this book, having a tea party in the American desert, meeting people from around the world. That is what I thought, anyway. Japan is a blast, isn't it! We are a race that can freeze water instantaneously (by adding one small stroke to the character for water changes the character's meaning to ice). That's all.

| | P036 | JPN | tel:06-6241-6048 fax:06-6241-6048
e-mail:kenhamazaki@hotmail.com

Vincent Huang
黄　文隆

Photographer

Profile

兵庫県神戸市生まれ。'82年、サンフレンスコ大学・アカデミーオブアートカレッジ写真科卒業。以後、写真家ヘルムートニュートンのアシスタントを経て、東京、NY、北京にてアート活動の傍ら、広告および映像の仕事に携わる。'88年、ADC広告美術年鑑マガジン部門受賞。

Born in Kobe. Graduated from the photo department of San Francisco University's Academy of Art College in 1982. Has since been assistant to the photographer Helmut Newton, been involved in art in Tokyo, New York, and Beijing, and worked in advertising and video. In 1988, he won a prize in the ADC Advertising Art Yearbook's magazine division.

Message

21世紀はアクエリアスの世紀である。私達のミッションは、全地球的、全生命的、全宇宙的な視点で、より美しい未来を創造していくことである。地球の美しさは、「そこだけに生命」があることからくるのだから…。

The 21st century is the century of Aquarius. Our mission is to create a more beautiful future, from a global, biologically diverse, universal perspective. The beauty of the Earth lies in the fact that all life depends upon it.

 P036 CHN　tel:03-3402-0428　fax:03-3402-0428
e-mail:vincent@jb3.so-net.ne.jp

Penguin no.1

Model

Profile

'97年、スドー・アート工房で、某社のCMキャラクターとして誕生。以後、冬眠期間を経て、「Water Planet」にアート作品のモデルとして参加。彼の故郷、スドー・アート工房からは、新潮文庫のCMキャラクターとして"Yonda?"も誕生している。

Made at Sudo Art Studio and got its start in 1997 as the promotional character for a certain company. After a period of hibernation, emerged as a model for an art piece in Water Planet. Sudo Art Studio also produced the commercial character "Yonda?" for the publisher Shincho Bunko.

Message

みんな、海をよごさないでネ。

Let's not pollute the sea, everyone, all right?

P006 JPN

Christopher Doyle

Photographer

Profile

今日まで12冊の本を出版し、写真、コラージュ、インスタレーションなどで数多くの個展やグループ展を催している。彼が映画監督としてデビューした作品の「AWAY WITH WORDS」は、'99のカンヌ映画祭にノミネートされ、世界中に公開された。

As well as publishing twelve books, Christopher Doyle has held numerous individual and group exhibitions of photography, collage, installation, and other works. "Away with Words," his first film as a director, was nominated for the Festival International du Film de Cannes 99 and shown around the world.

Message

「水」は私の作品の素となる、重用なファクターの一つです。私が集中して仕事する時は、いつも海の見える場所。つまり、海からエネルギーをもらえる場所にいます。

Water is one of the essential factors in my works. When I work intensively, I always choose a place where I can see the ocean. In other words, I'm always in a place where I can get energy from the ocean.

P048 AUS

How to order?

WATER PLANET STORE

■作品のご購入方法とご注意

お気に入りのアート作品は、少しでも早く手に入れたいもの。でも、「WATER PLANET STORE」では、いろんな作家の皆さんに直接作品を販売してもらうので、制作や販売のスタイルも様々。一般的な通販とは少しスタイルが違います。そこで、皆さんに安心してご利用いただくためにも、ご購入前にぜひ知っておいてもらいたいお約束をご紹介します。※販売エリアは、日本国内に限らせていただきます。

1 ご購入前に

「WATER PLANET STORE」で紹介される作品のほとんどが、限定ものなど、この本でしか買うことのできない作品です。しかも、他の通販雑誌などで販売される商品のように大量に生産されるものではありません。一点一点が作家の創作活動から生まれる貴重な作品。ですから、お届けするのに時間がかかったり、写真で見るものとは微妙に違っていたりすることがあるかも知れません。ご購入いただく方は、まずそのことをご理解ください。

2 作品購入の申し込み方法は?

掲載作品のご注文は、本誌付属の専用ハガキに必要事項をご記入の上お申し込みください。

3 「限定販売」&「受注制作」とは?

作品が既存の場合は「限定販売」。注文後に作品を制作するのが「受注制作」です。※「限定販売」は数に限りがあるため売り切れ次第、受付を終了いたします。また、「受注制作」は、作品をお送りするまでに多少日数がかかりますので予めご承知ください。

4 作品についての問い合わせは?

掲載作品ついてのお問い合わせについては、編集部では一切対応いたしませんのでご了承ください。

5 代金の支払い方法は?

代金の支払い方法は、ご購入お申し込み受付後に作家または販売代理店よりご連絡しますので指定の方法に従ってください。

6 送料はいるのでしょうか?

作品のご購入には、掲載されている作品の代金に加えて、送料及び梱包料が必要となります。なお送料及び梱包料は作家によって輸送システムが異なる上、地域、作品の大きさや重量などによって違いますのでご了承ください。また、一部の作品については消費税5%が必要となります。

7 作品は、いつ届くのでしょうか?

販売作品の納期は、作家及び作品ごとに異なりますが、受注制作によるハンドメイドの作品については、お送りするまで2週間〜1ヵ月程度かかりますのでご了承ください。

8

返品は可能でしょうか?

ご購入のお申し込みをされた作品のキャンセル及び、作品ご購入後の返品・お取り替えは、原則的にお断りいたします。

※やむをえずお客様のご都合でキャンセルされる場合は、キャセル料金が必要となる場合がありますのでご注意ください。なお、作家責任による作品の不良については、作品到着後に3日以内に作家までご連絡ください。

9

掲載作品の販売期間は?

本誌で掲載されている作品のご購入お申し込み受付は、平成12年6月20日(火)までです。それ以降は受付をいたしませんのでご了承ください。

■レシート表示の読み方

```
WATER PLANET STORE
purchasing information P.136

000-01  WATER PLANET  ¥1,900

01●素材／紙・水・ビニール ●サイズ／W00 D00
H00 ●セット内容／本・水・袋 ●限定00組 ※
送料込み
```

(A) WATER PLANET STOREのレシートがついている作品はすべてご購入いただけます。お申し込みハガキにレシートに記載の作品番号・作品名・価格・サイズ等をご記入ください。

(C) 表示の価格は作品の価格です。別途消費税が必要となる場合があります。

(D) サイズ(表示はmm単位、またM、L表示など)やカラーはお申し込みの際には必ずご記入ください。また限定販売、受注制作など各商品についての情報を記載しています。

(B) 頭の3桁は作家番号で、P.128〜P.135の作家紹介ページで作家情報をご覧いただけます。末の2桁は商品番号で、いずれもご購入申し込み時に必要となります。

■掲載の作品について

●掲載作品の多くはハンドメイドです。同じ作品でもカタチや表情が微妙に違いますのでご了承ください。
●掲載作品は、作家の都合で止む無く制作を中止することがありますのでご了承ください。
●印刷の都合上、色や質感が実際の作品と異なる場合がありますのでご了承ください。
●掲載作品の無断転載・複製を禁じます。

⚠ This application form is available until June 20 2000 only in Japan.
この作品購入の申し込みは平成12年6月20日まで有効です。
オーダーは日本国内のみ有効です。

DEEP SEA WATER POSTER GRANDPRIX 2000

出品募集概要 / Call for Entries

テーマ	「海洋深層水」をPRするポスター
作品規定	●B1タテ型（1030mm×728mm）限定。 ●シリーズ作品は不可。 ●ポスター紙面には必ず「DEEP SEA WATER」の文字を入れてください。 ●作品は未発表のものとし、使用するイラスト、写真、コピー等は全てオリジナルのものとします。 ●作品はウッドラックパネル（厚さ5mmか7mm）に貼り付けの上、ご提出ください。 ※既製の食品など商品を特定する表現の作品は、審査対象にはなりませんのでご注意ください。
参加資格	プロ・アマチュアを問わず、参加は自由です。
出品方法	下の出品応募用紙に必要事項を記入の上、出品作品の裏面左下スミに貼り付けて下記宛で先まで郵送してください。（作品が複数の場合は出品応募用紙をコピーしてお使いください）
出品点数	1人または1グループにつき、何点でも出品できます。
出品手数料	1点につき1,000円です。必ず出品点数分の出品手数料を入れた現金書留にて送付してください。その際、現金書留の控えを領収書に代えさせていただきます。 ※入金の確認できない場合は選考対象となりません。また、一度お納めいただいた出品手数料は返却いたしかねます。
出品応募先	〒542-0081　大阪市中央区南船場4-3-21森村御堂ビル4F GRAM INC.「海洋深層水ポスターグランプリ」事務局宛
募集締切	2000年5月10日（水）当日必着
審査・賞	東京アートディレクターズクラブに所属のクリエイター諸氏により審査の上、各賞を決定。 ●最優秀グランプリ賞 1名　●準グランプリ賞 2名 それぞれに表彰状と賞金を贈呈します。※賞金金額については未定。
発表	「WATER PLANET」第3号の誌面に、受賞作品及び作者を掲載のうえ、発表します。（なお、本誌関連のイベントにて優秀作品の展示を予定しております。）
作品の返却	応募された作品は一切返却いたしませんので、ご了承ください。
作品の著作権等	●作品の著作権・肖像権は、本グランプリ事務局に帰属します。 ●作品は未発表のものとし、表現及び使用する写真、イラスト等はオリジナルのものを使用してください。 ●著作権・肖像権等のトラブルについては、本誌編集部及び本グランプリ事務局は一切責任を持ちません。 ●上記の項目に違反する作品、また他人の諸権利に抵触する作品は、受賞後でも受賞資格を取り消す場合があります。

Theme : Poster to advertise Deep Sea Water
Poster contest rules : B-1 size, 1030mm x 728mm, landscape (horizontal) format. Single/individual images only; no diptychs, triptychs, etc. The phrase "DEEP SEA WATER" must appear in the poster. Works already published elsewhere are not acceptable. Illustrations, photographs, and bodycopy must be original. Submissions should be on foam core panel of 5-7 mm thickness. Works which feature specific products will not be accepted.
Qualification : Open to all entrants. Professional and amateur alike.
Entry procedure : Please fill-out the entry form which comes with this magazine and attach it to the bottom left corner of the reverse side of your entry and send it to the following address: If you submit more than one entry, please photocopy the entry form.
Number of entries : You may submit as many entries as you like.
Submission fee : The fee is 1,000 yen per entry. Please send your total submission fee in cash by registered mail. Please keep your registered mail receipt as proof of payment. Your entry is not official until we receive your entry fee. Entry fees are non-refundable.
Address : Gram, Inc.
"Deep Sea Water Gran Prix"Contest Entry Department
Morimuramido Bldg. 4F 4-3-21 Minamisenba
Chou-ku Osaka 542-0081 Japan
Deadline for entries : Must be received by: Wednesday, May 10, 2000, Japan Standard Time
Judgement and Award: The poster contest will be judged by members of the Tokyo Art Directors' Club. One Grand Prize winner will be declared and presented with a certificate of commendation and prize-money. Second Prize: two winners will receive a certificate of commendation and prize-money. Prize money to be announced at a later date.
Announcement : The winner will be announced in the third issue of WATER PLANET with pictures of the winning entry and the artist. We are also planning to exhibit the Grand Prix winner at other promotional events.
Return of entries : All entries become the property of WATER PLANET and will not be returned.
Copyrights : All entries and copyrights become the property of WATER PLANET upon submission to this contest. All images and body copy of entries must be original and previously unpublished. Our editorial and Gran Prix departments are not responsible for any copyright disputes or problems. Works which violate any of the previously mentioned contest rules, or conflict with any prior copyrights will be disqualified.

- - - - - - キ リ ト リ - - - - - -

DEEP SEA WATER POSTER GRANDPRIX 2000

応　募　用　紙
Entry form

氏 名 / Name		年 齢 /Age	職 業 / Occupation
グループの場合は代表者名 /If a group, please write the representative's name.			
住 所 / Address			
T E L（自宅・会社） / Telephone number (home / work)		整理番号（主催者の記入欄です） reference number / official use only	

PRESENT

本誌に付属のアンケートハガキにお答えいただいた方の中から抽選で、素敵なプレゼントを差し上げます。

We will hold a drawing from the opinion survey submissions, and some lucky people will win a present!

VISIONAIRE NO.30
presented by hacknet

話題を呼んだルイ・ヴィトンの第2弾。テーマは「GAME」。キューブを合わせると作品になる。オーストラリアで開催のルイ・ヴィトン・カップに参加する7ヵ国のヴァージョンがあり、国旗がモチーフのケースには、それぞれの国を代表するアーティストが作品を提供している。7タイプから、いずれかを2名様に。

This is the second magazine sponcered by Louis Vuitton. It will get into the news. The theme is "game". When you put the cubes together, it becomes a product. There are seven countries' versions which compete in the Louis Vuitton Cup held in Australia. The motif of the case is each country's flag. Artists from each country submit work. We will give two lucky people this magazine.

Ken Hamazaki & Vincent Huang
original T-shirt & poster

「バーニング・マン」で、日本代表としてパフォーマンスを披露してくれたケン・ハマザキとヴィンセント・ホアンの2人から、オリジナルポスターを20名様に。また、赤い水が入ったビニールポケットの付いたTシャツを1名様に。いずれも本誌でしか手に入れることのできない非売品です。

Original posters by Ken Hamazaki and Vincent Huang, who participated at Burning Man, will be awarded to 20 lucky repondents to our questionnaire. In addition, a T-shirt with a vinyl, red-colored water-filled pocket will be presented to one lucky person. The T-shirt and posters are limited edition works unavailable anywhere else.

プレゼント当選者の発表は、
賞品の発送をもって代えさえ
ていただきます。
締切日/平成12年6月20日
Deadlinde/June 20th, 2000

INFORMATION

call for participation

本誌では、「水」をテーマにした作品を募集しております。参加ご希望の方は作品の資料（写真等）及び作家ご本人のプロフィールを下記宛て先まで郵送またはE-mailでお送りください。編集部にて選考いたします。（お送りいただいた資料は返却いたしませんのでご了承ください。）
●海外アーティストに詳しいコーディネーターの方は、ぜひ情報をお寄せください。

WATER PLANET is soliciting work with the theme of "WATER". Any submissions in this category are welcome. Please send any submissions, along with the artist's profile to the following address or contact us by email at:waterplanet@pictogram.co.jp The editorial department will make selections from all submissions received. We cannot return any submissions. Foreign artists' agents may also submit work on their clients' behalf.

www.pictogram.co.jp

本誌記事以外の情報がホームページでご覧いただけます。

Our homepage shows additional information about features in this book.

recruit new staff

「WATER PLANET」では、スタッフを募集しています。
①CD（企画営業）②グラフィックデザイナー
①は出版・広告業界での営業経験5年以上
②はグラフィックデザイナーとしてのデザイン経験3年以上
いずれも専門・短大卒以上で30歳ぐらいまでの方。
履歴書（写真貼付）に業務経験内容をできるだけ詳しく明記の上、郵送ください。書類選考の上、追って面接日をご連絡いたします。※連絡可能な時間帯と電話番号をご記入ください。
※締切日/平成12年4月10日

next issue 2000.6.20

次号は水の色を変えて本年6月20日に発売予定です。
お楽しみに。

The second of WATER PLANET is scheduled to be published on June 20th, 2000.

PICTO inc. 大阪市中央区南船場4-3-21
森村御堂ビル4F 〒542-0081
4F Morimuramido Bldg, 4-3-21 Minamisenba,
Chuo-ku, Osaka 542-0081JAPAN
e-mail waterplanet@pictogram.co.jp

c o l l a b o r a t o r s

● **photographer**
Yasushi Nakamura (P4~7, P12~15, P23, P56, P57, P76~81, P87~90,
P105, P114, P116, P117)
Nob Fukuda (P9~11, P27~35, P54, P55, P62, P92, P96~104, P115)
Shinji Ashizawa (P58~61, P64~75, P82, P120, P121)
Mieko Mizushima (P107~113)
Masato Ishimoto (P13)

● **writer**
Yuko Sato (P22~29, P34, P35, P87~91, P104, P105, P114~117)
Yuka Kinba (P36~45)
Kimiko Yamada (P30, P31, P48, P50, P84, P85, P102, P103, P116)

● **stylist**
Seiji Sageshima (P14, P15, P76~81)
Noriko Tanaka (P14, P15, P76~81, P87~90)

● **food art**
Ikuko Mizushima (P9, P34, P35)

● **penguin**
Sudo Art Kobo (P6)

● **illustration**
Piroro / Idoking / Fancy shop furuchan

s p e c i a l   t h a n k s

Koichi Ozaki / Shingo Sugimoto / Shinobu Mochizuki
Yusuke Kanou / Sumiyo Otsuki / Yukihiro Kusaka
Miyuki Nishida / Nananin / Saeko Nishimura
Masayo Ogawa / Keiko Sakata / Hiroshi Narasaki
Katsuyuki Taniuchi / Junko Ohtsuka / Hiroko Hosomi
Tomoyuki Tanaka / Tokiko Sato / Chiyae Maedomari
Hidetoshi Nakamoto / SEMPRE DESIGN
Daisuke Yoshida / Michiko Ohno / Katsuya Ishida
Kazuko Takeda / XANADEUX CO.,LTD
Chifuyu Miyaji / HACK NET / BESPOKE TAILOR DMG
Shinobu Masuda / Shigeki Hattori

WATER PLANET 01

発行日	2000年2月20日
発行者	GRAM INC.
	大阪市中央区南船場4-3-21森村御堂ビル4F
	〒542-0081 tel.06 6258 9490 fax.06 6241 5554
発売元	MEMEX INC.
	大阪市中央区南船場4-9-8
	〒542-0081 tel.06 6281 2828 fax.06 6258 4440
編集・企画	PICTO INC.
アートディレクション	ヤマモトヒロユキ
デザイン	井戸木智仁・荻田純・古川智基
コピー	藤本健嗣
コーディネーション	片桐由貴
セールスプロモーション	安岡洋一
翻訳	国沢郁子・Richard S. Sheridan
印刷・製本	大日本印刷株式会社
定価	本体￥1,900（税別）
	ISBN4-907802-00-5 C9476 ￥1900E

the date of issue	February 20.2000
published by	GRAM INC.
	4F Morimuramido Bldg, 4-3-21 Minamisenba,
	Chuo-ku, Osaka JAPAN
	tel. +81 6 6258 9490 fax. +81 6 6241 5554
distributed by	MEMEX INC.
	4-9-8 Minamisenba, Chuo-ku, Osaka JAPAN
	tel. +81 6 6281 2828 fax. +81 6 6258 4440
edited by	PICTO INC.
art director	Hiroyuki Yamamoto
designer	Tomohito Idoki / Jun Ogita / Tomoki Furukawa
copy writer	Kenji Fujimoto
coordinator	Yuki Katagiri
sales promoter	Yoichi Yasuoka
translator	Ikuko Kunizawa / Richard S. Sheridan
printed by	Dai Nippon Printing Co., Ltd.
	ISBN4-907802-00-5 C9476 ￥1900E

ホンジツノ オカイアゲ.........ショウケイ　¥2,656,300
　　　　　　　　　　　　　　　ゼイ　　　¥132,815

　　　　　　　　　　　　ゴウケイ　¥2,789,115